IT'S YOUR PLANET

GO SCIENCE!

Berry Billingsley • Rob Butler
William Lynn • Dave Mason
Nigel Saunders • Nicole Sloane
Philip Smith • Sian van der Welle

Series editor:
Byron Dawson

BOOK **2**

D0306455

www.heinemann.co.uk

✓ Free online support
✓ Useful weblinks
✓ 24 hour online ordering

01865 888118

Contents

Key to focus on how science works symbols

 investigation

analysing data

science in the news

science and the world around us

Contents

How to use this book

Welcome to *Go Science!* We believe that learning about science, what scientists do and how science works should be fun. So we've packed in lots of amazing photos and illustrations, foul facts and interesting facts, as well as different types of exciting pages including 'setting the scene', 'focus on how science works' and the 'best science lessons ever'.

Here are the main types of pages in *Go Science!*

These are the 'setting the scene' pages. They tell you what you are going to be learning about in the chapter.

Here are some questions to get your brain warmed up before you get into the main lessons.

Read about the illustration. If you have the **LiveText CD-ROM**, you will be able to click on 'hotspots' around the photo to discover more.

These photos and captions give you some clues about what is coming up in the chapter. If you have the **LiveText CD-ROM**, you will be able to click on these photos and find out more.

Questions in the text make sure you have understood what you have just read. They are colour coded and the levels are in brackets, so you know what level you're working at.

This is one of the main lessons. This box tells you what you will be learning about in the lesson.

Foul facts are about the 'yucky' parts of science.

The keyword box lists all the keywords in a lesson. If you have the **LiveText CD-ROM** you can click on the glossary word and a pop-up box will give you its definition.

Key to question colours

Level 4	Level 6
Level 5	Level 7

In this 'focus on how science works' lesson you will look at some real scientific research

Using real scientific data will help you make your own mind up about the science.

You can read different people's views and make up your own mind.

We asked you what you liked most about science and many of you said it was the practicals, so we've included some 'best science lessons ever' in the book.

Here's a step-by-step guide to what you will be doing in the practical.

At the end of the book, there are two science skills spreads that tell you about science in the media and how to write about science.

On the **LiveText CD-ROM**, there are six extension lessons that don't appear in this book. These help you practise your scientific skills.

Here's a list of what equipment you will need.

At the end there are some questions for you to answer.

The *Go Science!* pupils

Ryan

Becca

Jasmine

Amber

Sam

London 2012. Are you going to be there? Tom Daley certainly hopes to be. Having won six gold medals in Manchester at the British Diving Championship in 2008 at the age 13, Tom has his sights set on the Olympic dream. But for Tom to achieve his goal there will be a team of people behind him, many of them scientists, as he strives to be the best in the world.

Athletes in the first Olympic Games held in Athens nearly 2800 years ago ate fish and cheese followed by figs for lunch. We now know much more about how our bodies work. We also know how the diets of different athletes in different sports need to be adjusted to suit them.

IDEAL (Institute of Diet, Exercise and Lifestyle) at the University of Glasgow looks at exercise and diet to improve performance. Having a good diet is important for everyone, but for serious sportsmen and women it can be the difference between winning and losing.

When athletes perform, their bodies must work at their very best. Sports scientists give athletes advice on diet, exercise and education. As our understanding of sport science increases so the performance of athletes improves.

Now try these

- What is the name of the organ that pumps blood to every part of the body?

- When athletes compete, who else is involved in their effort to do their very best?

- In order to stay healthy, which foods shouldn't you eat too much of?

- What might happen to you if you do eat too much of these foods?

Coming up in this Chapter ...

Healthy diets help us grow healthy

Sweets often contain colourings and flavourings

Plants use sunlight to make their food

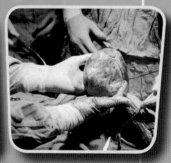

Good food keeps your heart healthy

Learn about:

- what nutrients are found in food
- why a balanced diet is important
- how doctors discovered how to prevent scurvy
- using evidence to support an idea

Interesting fact

Hildegard von Bingen was born in Germany in 1098. In 1150, she wrote a book on the natural sciences called *Causae et Curae*. In it she said that only by eating the right plant or animal could a healthy balance be obtained in the body. Some people think she was one of the first dieticians.

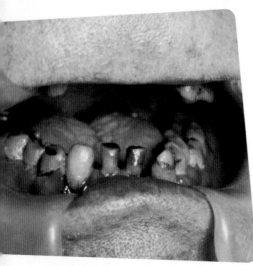

▲ Scurvy is a horrible disease that can take up to six months to kill you

For many people in the world, starvation is a danger that never goes away. In the West there is always plenty to eat. Some people eat too much food but others don't eat enough.

Eating yourself healthy

Nutrients are the substances in food that your body needs to be healthy. A diet that has just the right amount of nutrients is called a **balanced diet**. **Nutritionists** are scientists who study diet. They work out exactly what is in our food. They have identified five important types of nutrients:

- **carbohydrates** and **fats** which give you energy
- **proteins** that help your body to grow and repair itself
- **vitamins** and **minerals** which are needed in small amounts.

Although they are not nutrients, water and **fibre** are also needed. Fibre keeps the food moving through your gut and stops you being constipated. Water is needed for all the chemical reactions in your body to take place in.

A (i) What types of nutrients give you energy? (ii) What does your body need protein for? (Level 4)

A deadly killer

If your diet is missing even one important nutrient then you can become very ill. Between the seventeenth and nineteenth centuries, **scurvy** killed one million British sailors. Their legs had ulcers, they bled from their eyes and their teeth dropped out. Then they went blind. Scars would reopen, seeping pus, and eventually they would die.

Science to the rescue

In 1747, Dr James Lind was a ship's doctor on board HMS Salisbury. He looked at the sailors with scurvy and thought they were 'rotting'. Dr Lind thought about what he could do to stop the 'rotting'. He knew pickling onions in acids like vinegar stopped rotting. He linked these two **observations** to make a **hypothesis**.

B (i) What was Dr Lind's hypothesis? (ii) Explain what Dr Lind needed to do to turn his hypothesis into a theory. (Level 5)

To find out if an acid could stop the rotting, he conducted an experiment. He selected 12 sailors with scurvy. He then selected sulfuric acid and five other things that contained acid: vinegar, cider, barley water, oranges and lemons.

He divided the 12 sailors into pairs. One of each pair ate or drank one of the acidic substances. The other from each pair did not. To make it a fair test, everything they ate and drank, other than the acid substances, was the same.

C Explain why Dr Lind's work was a scientific experiment. (Level 5)

D Design a table in which Dr Lind could record which diet resulted in a cure for scurvy and which did not. (Level 6)

Dr Lind's results

After only five days, those eating the fruit recovered. The others showed no improvement. Dr Lind could see a pattern in his results. Using this evidence, he made the following theory: 'The acid in fruit is a cure for scurvy.'

My name is Sonja and I work with sprinters as a sports scientist. As well as understanding how the body moves, I need to know how the body reacts to different types of exercise and different environments. I also need to study diet and nutrition.

▲ These fruits all contain acid

E We now know it is a lack of vitamin C that causes scurvy and that vitamin C cures it. Why do scientists still respect and study Dr Lind's work? (Level 7)

Keywords
anorexia, balanced diet, carbohydrate, fat, fibre, hypothesis, mineral, nutrient, nutritionist, obese, observations, protein, scurvy, vitamin

Learn about:

- what a food additive is and how they are used
- the food additive debate
- evidence can refute or support an argument

Are E numbers safe for kids?
Shocking new scientific evidence reveals that E numbers can harm children.

Ingredients

Sugar, Wheat Flour, Water, Colours (E150c, E162, E160a, E100), Liquorice extract, Citric acid, Humectant (E422), Stabilisers (E414, E413), Salt, Dextrose, Flavourings, Emulsifier (E471)

Contains sulfur dioxide and traces of soya.

 The ingredients of Jumbo Juicy Bears

A Ingredients are always listed with the main ingredient first. Look at the ingredients of Jumbo Juicy Bears. What is the main ingredient of this sweet? (Level 4)

What is a food additive?

Food additives are substances added to foods by food manufacturers. They put different additives into foods for different reasons – to colour them, to flavour them and to preserve them.

It takes years of tests for an additive to be declared safe. When an additive has passed these safety tests it is given an **E number**, for example E100 or E101. The safety of food additives is constantly being checked as scientists find new evidence about their effects on humans.

B How many E numbers are there in Jumbo Juicy Bears? (Level 4)

Scientists argue

In September 2007, when scientists reported a link between food additives and temper tantrums in children, it was headline news. The scientists said that their experiment showed differences in the children's behaviour when they drank fruit drinks that contained a mixture of food colourings and preservatives. They wanted a review of the laws on what could be put into children's food.

▶ Many food additives come in powder form

Foul Fact

Ancient Romans used to sweeten their wine with lead. They did not know that lead is a poison. Many Romans became ill or even died as a result.

Some scientists said that the results were very important and the experiment was a good one. Other scientists disagreed with their findings.

C Some scientists say that everything can do you harm if you eat too much of it. What do you need to know to make sure your diet is healthy? (Level 5)

The government has advised parents of children with poor behaviour that they might think about cutting food additives from their children's diet. Food manufacturers have said that they are trying to reduce the number of additives in their products.

D Scientists are still arguing about whether or not additives cause bad behaviour. But food manufacturers have said that they are going to reduce the number of additives anyway. Why do you think this is? (Level 6)

What do you think?

Some people will eat almost anything. It is not the job of scientists to tell people what to eat. All scientists can do is present people with the evidence from their experiments. It is up to people what they do then. Some people do not eat meat, some will eat only fruit and nuts, and others will only eat foods after a religious leader has said that the food is acceptable.

Arthur Boyt of Cornwall likes to eat roadkill – dead animals that he finds at the side of the road. He eats everything including the eyeballs. Most people, though, look to scientists to tell them that their food is safe. This means that scientific evidence can have a big impact on people's lives.

▲ Roadkill for lunch!

E Why do you think that some people listen to what religious leaders have to say about food, when those leaders may have no scientific training? (Level 7)

Keywords
E number, food additive

7

Learn about:

- how doctors discovered how digestion breaks down food
- why scientists need to think 'is this ethical?' when they are designing experiments
- how ethics can influence how scientists work

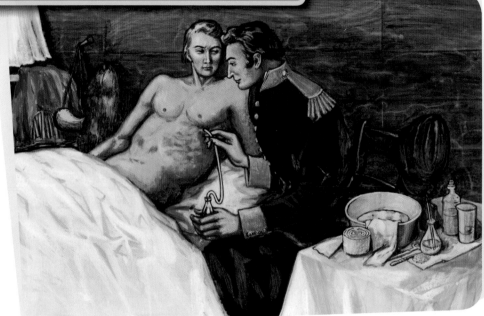

▲ Is it right for scientists to experiment on humans?

When Alexis St Martin was shot in 1822 he thought he was going to die. The blast left a hole in his side and his breakfast was oozing out. Dr William Beaumont helped Alexis recover but the wound healed leaving a hole the size of a 10 pence piece.

Experimenting on humans

Through the hole, people could see inside Alexis St Martin's **stomach**. In 1822, no one knew exactly what went on in the stomach. So, rather than close up the hole, Dr Beaumont gave Alexis a servant's job and did hundreds of experiments on him.

Dr Beaumont became rich and famous for his discoveries. He pushed meat through the hole into the stomach and then took it out and examined it. He repeated the experiment with different foods and took samples of the **digestive juices**. When Alexis became angry because of the pain, Dr Beaumont observed that anger slowed down the rate of **digestion**.

The digestive system

When you eat your food, it starts a journey through a pipe that is over 8 m long. This pipe is called the **gut**. It is part of the **digestive system**, which consists of all the organs concerned with digestion.

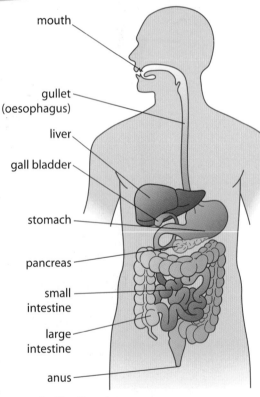

mouth

gullet (oesophagus)

liver

gall bladder

stomach

pancreas

small intestine

large intestine

anus

▲ The digestive system

Foul Fact

Lazzaro Spallanzani (1729–1799) was an Italian doctor who kept vomit for several hours and discovered that food carried on being digested.

A Look at the diagram of the digestive system. Name the parts of the gut that link the mouth to the stomach and the stomach to the large intestine. (Level 4)

As food travels through the gut, it is broken down into smaller and smaller pieces until the particles are small enough to be absorbed into the body. The stomach's job is to take chewed food and turn it into a runny soup-like liquid. It really is a bag of sick.

Enzymes

With the evidence from the experiments on Alexis's stomach, Dr Beaumont discovered the speed of the chemical breakdown of different foods. The mouth, stomach and **small intestine** add chemicals called **enzymes**. These help to speed up the breakdown of the foods into very small particles. They work best at body temperature and, without them, digestion would take days, not hours.

The small particles are then absorbed through the wall of the small intestine and into the blood. The wall of the small intestine is like a sieve, letting small particles through into the blood but keeping large particles out. You can see how this works in the diagram.

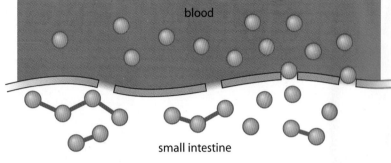
blood

small intestine

▲ Large food particles such as proteins are broken down into smaller food particles that can be absorbed by the body

> Forensic scientists, nurses, dieticians and some teachers have qualifications in physiology.

B The digestive system is involved in the digestion of food. Name two other systems in your body and what is involved in each. (Level 5)

Is it right?

Dr Beaumont was always keen to describe his discoveries but we don't know whether he ever asked Alexis about how he felt about being experimented on.

Dr Beaumont invented the science of **physiology** which studies the chemical reactions and biological functions in the body. Today, physiology is a major part of medicine. All doctors study it to help them cure many patients and diseases.

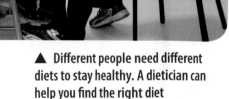

▲ Different people need different diets to stay healthy. A dietician can help you find the right diet

C Suggest a model to describe the action of enzymes on large food particles. (Level 6)

D The results of Dr Beaumont's research have benefited millions of people. Was Dr Beaumont right to experiment on one person so that many others would benefit? List arguments that support and arguments that oppose his work. (Level 7)

Keywords
digestion, digestive juices, digestive system, enzyme, gut, physiology, small intestine, stomach

1.5 GUT-WRENCHING DIGESTION

Learn about:
- how a model can show how food is broken down in the digestive system

▶ If you are what you eat, why don't you look like this bread?

Best Science Lesson Ever

Imagine you can see inside your digestive system. What happens to the food that you eat? How does your body break down your meals to get the useful nutrients? You are going to use everyday items to model how the structures in your digestive system function and work together. You will see what happens to a school dinner as it passes through your body.

A List the parts of the digestive system from mouth to anus. (Level 4)

What you will need

You will need to organise yourselves into groups of four. For each group, you will need:

- a school dinner
- a mouth – pestle and mortar
- a stomach – clear, sealable plastic bag
- an intestine – leg of tights
- enzymes (**amylase**, **protease**, **lipase**) – labelled bottles of liquid
- stomach acid – labelled bottle of liquid

What to do

1 Grind up your dinner in the mouth (pestle and mortar). Add a few drops of amylase.

2  When you've ground up your dinner enough, pour it into the stomach (plastic bag). Add a few drops of stomach acid and protease.

3  Squidge the contents of the bag with your hands. Cut the corner of the bag and squeeze the contents into the small intestine (thin, top end of tights). Add a few drops of lipase.

4 Push the food along with your hands so that it passes through the intestine. Watch how the 'digested nutrients' pass through the wall.

5 Continue to squeeze the contents through the large intestine (thick, foot end of tights). Watch how the remaining water passes through the walls.

6 Once you have reached the end of the large intestine (the toe of the tights), cut the end off with a pair of scissors. Squeeze out the undigested remains. Yuk!

B Why do the mouth and stomach both squeeze and break up the food? (Level 5)

C The adult intestine is approximately 7.5 metres long and surrounded by a very rich blood supply. Suggest why. (Level 6)

D Food is pushed through the digestive system by muscle contractions. How do you show this in your model? (Level 7)

Keywords
amylase, lipase, protease

Voted a Best Lesson at The John Warner School, Hoddesdon

Learn about:

- aerobic and anaerobic respiration
- how plants respire and how they capture energy

▲ Athletes like Andy Murray take great care what they eat to improve their performance

As a sportsman, Andy Murray needs lots of energy. He gets his energy mainly from carbohydrates, which are found in bread, potatoes and pasta. As Andy says, 'I eat a lot of pasta.'

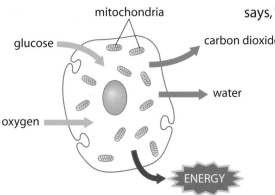

▲ Aerobic respiration in a cell

A What type of nutrient should you get most of your energy from? (Level 4)

Energy from food

The carbohydrates in food are digested to produce **glucose**. Glucose is the body's fuel. Using glucose in your body to release energy is called **respiration** and it happens in every one of your cells.

There are two kinds of respiration: **aerobic respiration** and **anaerobic respiration**. Aerobic respiration needs a fuel (glucose) and oxygen from the air, just like burning. It produces carbon dioxide and water as waste products.

B Compare aerobic respiration with burning by writing two word equations, one for each type of reaction. (Level 5)

Feel the burn

When you exercise you need even more energy so your muscles respire more than usual. You feel hot as your body burns more fuel. You breathe faster and your heart pounds as you increase the supply of glucose and oxygen to your muscles for aerobic respiration.

▲ Regular exercise increases your body's ability to supply glucose and oxygen to your cells and take away the waste products of carbon dioxide and water

Sometimes you can't get enough oxygen to your cells because the demand for energy is too great. Your cells can then use anaerobic respiration for a short time. Anaerobic respiration can release energy without oxygen but it produces a toxic substance called **lactic acid**. Too much lactic acid is poisonous and causes your muscles to ache and stop working.

Plants respire too

All living cells need energy to carry out their life processes. Just like animal cells, plant cells also need to respire. They use glucose and oxygen to make carbon dioxide and water and to release energy.

Jasmine and Sam plan an experiment to find out about plant respiration. Some indicators change colour with carbon dioxide. They set up two test tubes, half full with red indicator solution – one with mung beans on a wire grid and one with just the wire grid. 'If the beans are respiring,' said Jasmine, 'then the indicator in the test tube with the beans will change colour as they produce carbon dioxide.'

Plants can't move and they don't feel warm, so why do they need to respire?

But plants do reproduce and grow.

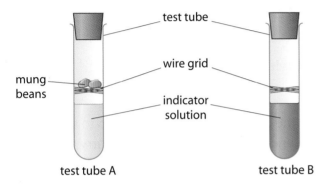

test tube

wire grid

mung beans

indicator solution

test tube A

test tube B

◀ Jasmine and Sam's experiment after it has been left for a day

C Look at Jasmine and Sam's experiment. Compare the colour of the indicator in each test tube. (i) Why do you think the indicator changes colour? (ii) Does the evidence support Jasmine's prediction? (Level 6)

Plant food

Plants don't eat food, so where do they get their glucose? Plants carry out a process called **photosynthesis**. A chemical in their leaves called **chlorophyll** captures energy from sunlight. Plants use this energy plus carbon dioxide from the air and water to produce glucose and oxygen. Then they use this glucose to respire. Just like animal cells, plant cells respire all the time. Unlike animal cells, they can make glucose and oxygen when there is sunlight. Plants also need nutrients from the soil to survive.

Take a look at the word equations for respiration and photosynthesis.

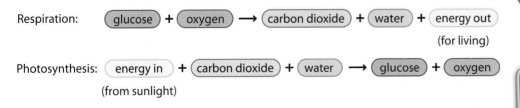

Respiration: glucose + oxygen ⟶ carbon dioxide + water + energy out
(for living)

Photosynthesis: energy in + carbon dioxide + water ⟶ glucose + oxygen
(from sunlight)

Scientists at work

Jan Ingenhousz was a Dutch scientist in the eighteenth century who discovered photosynthesis. He proved that plants take in water and carbon dioxide and give off oxygen. He later showed that this only happened when the plant was in daylight.

Keywords
aerobic respiration, anaerobic respiration, chlorophyll, glucose, lactic acid, photosynthesis, respiration

D Explain why plants need animals just as much as animals need plants, even though plants both respire and photosynthesise. (Level 7)

Swiss Cottage
St. John's Wood
Mornington Crescent
King's Cross
St. Pancras
Highbury & Islington
Great Portland
Baker
Euston
Angel
'are

1.7 The body's transport system

aster Bond Street
ite
Oxford Circus
Street
Holborn
Chancery Lane
St. Paul's
Aldga Eas
Marble Arch
Tottenham Court Road
Covent Garden ◆
Bank
Aldgate
lyde Park Corner
Green Park
Piccadilly Circus
Leicester Square
Mansion House
Cannon Street
Monument
Tower Hill
Tower Gateway
Ige
Charing Cross
Open Mondays - Fridays until 2100 only Saturdays 0730 - 1930
Fenchurch Street 150m
Sloane Square
St. James's Park
Blackfriars
River Thames
Victoria
Westminster
Temple
Embankment
Charing Cross 100m
London Bridge
Rotherhi
Bermondsey Ca

Learn about:

- how the circulatory system works
- how ideas about the circulatory system have changed over time

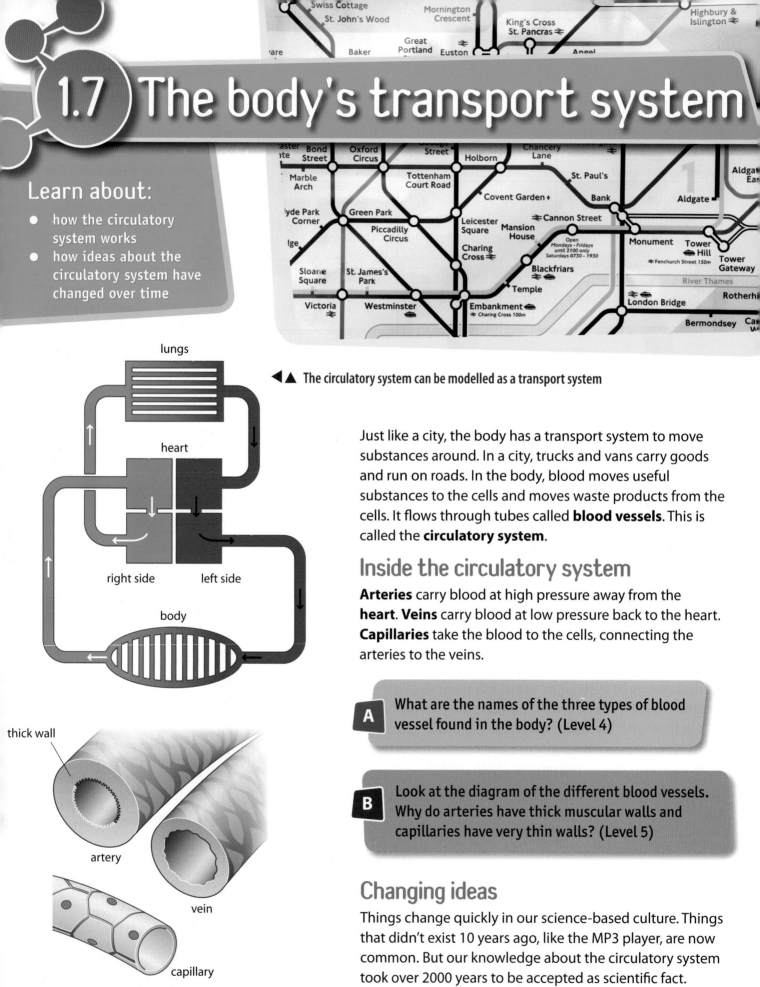

lungs

heart

right side   left side

body

▲◀ The circulatory system can be modelled as a transport system

Just like a city, the body has a transport system to move substances around. In a city, trucks and vans carry goods and run on roads. In the body, blood moves useful substances to the cells and moves waste products from the cells. It flows through tubes called **blood vessels**. This is called the **circulatory system**.

Inside the circulatory system

Arteries carry blood at high pressure away from the **heart**. **Veins** carry blood at low pressure back to the heart. **Capillaries** take the blood to the cells, connecting the arteries to the veins.

thick wall

artery

vein

capillary

▲ The different blood vessels

A What are the names of the three types of blood vessel found in the body? (Level 4)

B Look at the diagram of the different blood vessels. Why do arteries have thick muscular walls and capillaries have very thin walls? (Level 5)

Changing ideas

Things change quickly in our science-based culture. Things that didn't exist 10 years ago, like the MP3 player, are now common. But our knowledge about the circulatory system took over 2000 years to be accepted as scientific fact.

Aristotle

Erasistratus

Galen

Ibn-al-Nafis

Leonardo da Vinci

Leeuwenhoek

1 **Greece (around 400 BC)** Aristotle dissects animals to discover two types of blood vessels: veins and arteries.

2 **Egypt (300 BC)** Erasistratus predicts that invisible blood vessels must join them but, as no-one can see them, this can't be proved.

3 **Rome (200 AD)** Galen shows that blood in arteries and veins is a different colour.

4 **Syria (1242)** Ibn-al-Nafis observes that the blood goes from the heart to the lungs and back to the heart before going round the body.

5 **Italy (1510)** Leonardo da Vinci discovers capillaries.

6 **Holland (1688)** Leeuwenhoek uses the microscope to see blood travelling through capillaries.

C List each scientist mentioned above and explain whether their contribution to our understanding was from observation, experiment or prediction. (Level 6)

Just a heartbeat

You can feel the heart pumping the blood round your body by taking your pulse. If your heart stops, you will be unconscious in two minutes and dead within four.

D Why do we die if our heart stops beating? (Level 6)

If for any reason the blood vessels to a part of your body get blocked, all the cells supplied by those blood vessels die. If the area is large enough you get gangrene, as your flesh rots while it is still attached to you.

Interesting fact

The heart pumps about 80 ml of blood with every beat. If an adult heart were connected to a road tanker it would fill it in a single day.

▶ Limbs with gangrene may need to be amputated

E Imagine that you are a medical scientist. Describe an experiment you could do on some tissue to prove it is dead. What results would you expect? (Level 7)

Keywords
artery, blood vessel, capillary, circulatory system, heart, vein

1.8 Every breath you take

Learn about:
- how and why you breathe
- why scientists analyse breath

▶ Free divers can hold their breath for much longer than most people

> How long can you hold your breath for? 20 seconds? 40 seconds? A minute? Eventually, no matter how fit you are, you will have to take a breath.

Free diving is a sport where people see how deep they can go underwater, and get back, without breathing. The world records in 2007 were 214 m for men, held by the Austrian Herbert Nitsch, and 160 m for women, held by Tanya Streeter who is from the Caribbean. The UK free diving champion, Hannah Stacey, can hold her breath for an amazing four and a half minutes.

As you read these words, you are breathing. Put your hands on your sides and feel your chest gently rising and falling. During your life you will probably take about six hundred million breaths. That's a lot of breaths.

A Name the process taking place in your body that is using up oxygen and producing carbon dioxide. (Level 4)

Breathe in

You need to breathe because the cells in your body continually respire, using oxygen and producing carbon dioxide. Laid out flat, your **lungs** have the surface area of a tennis court. This area is so large because the lungs have lots of tiny air sacs called **alveoli**. Their walls are moist, very thin and have a network of tiny blood vessels that surrounds each sac.

When we breathe:
- oxygen from the air dissolves in the moisture lining the alveoli
- they then **diffuse** through the air sac walls and into the surrounding blood vessels
- the blood then takes the oxygen to all the cells of the body
- the cells produce carbon dioxide as a waste product
- carbon dioxide diffuses into the blood from the cells
- the blood carries the carbon dioxide to the lungs, where it diffuses across the walls of the blood vessels into the alveoli
- carbon dioxide is then breathed out.

Interesting fact

You breathe over 350,000 cubic metres of air in your life. This is nearly five times more than the world's largest hot-air balloon. This balloon is so big it could hold a jumbo jet without the wings or body touching its walls.

The movement of oxygen out of the alveoli and of carbon dioxide into the alveoli is called **gas exchange**. Your lungs and all the tubes are part of an organ system called the **respiratory system**.

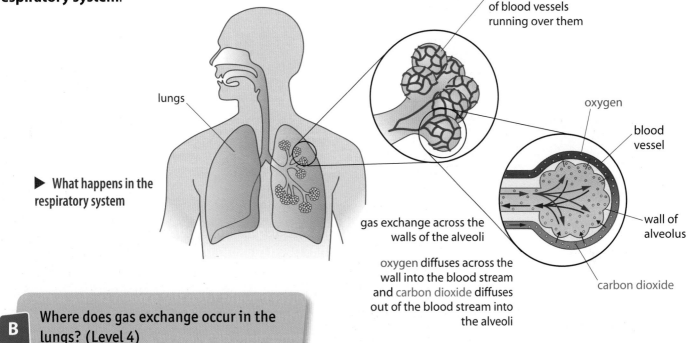

alveoli with networks of blood vessels running over them

lungs

oxygen

blood vessel

gas exchange across the walls of the alveoli

wall of alveolus

oxygen diffuses across the wall into the blood stream and carbon dioxide diffuses out of the blood stream into the alveoli

carbon dioxide

▶ What happens in the respiratory system

B Where does gas exchange occur in the lungs? (Level 4)

Catch your breath

Gina works as a physiologist. She says, 'The air we breathe in is different from the air we breathe out. We have analysed these differences and have produced this table of data.'

Doctors can use this data to compare the air breathed in and out by patients. This helps them diagnose their patients' problems. Sports scientists also use this table and data from other experiments to help free divers and other athletes improve their performance.

How the composition of the air breathed in is different from the air breathed out		
Gas	In air breathed in (%)	In air breathed out (%)
nitrogen	79	79
oxygen	20	15
carbon dioxide	0.04	4

D Using your bar chart and the data table above, explain the difference between the levels of oxygen and carbon dioxide in the composition of the air you breathe out and the air you breathe in. (Level 6)

C Using the data table above, draw a bar chart showing the difference between air breathed in and air breathed out. (Level 5)

E Imagine you are an oxygen atom. Explain what happens from the moment you are inhaled as part of an oxygen molecule to when you are exhaled as part of a water molecule. (Level 7)

Keywords
alveoli, diffuse, gas exchange, lungs, respiratory system

1.9 Displaying your data

Learn about:

- using and analysing charts and graphs

▲ Fertilisers supply plants with important nutrients

Runner bean experiment

The runner bean plants are grown in separate pots, each of which has a different fertiliser added. The pots are kept in a line on the windowsill so that they each receive the same amount of sunlight. The plants are watered every day with the same amount of water. After several weeks, Amber, Jasmine and Ryan measure the heights of the runner bean plants. The table below shows their results.

Average height of the runner bean plants	
Type of fertiliser	Average height
No fertiliser	15
Amber's Gran's	27
Natto's own brand	23
Sailbury's own brand	24
Brill Grow Plant Food	25

Amber's Gran is a keen gardener and she swears by her own fertiliser. She has been making this the same way for many years.

Ryan doesn't believe that homemade fertiliser can be that good and says that fertiliser bought from the garden centre is the best. Jasmine suggests that they conduct an experiment to prove who is right. 'By comparing three different brands of fertiliser with Amber's Gran's own variety,' she says, 'we can find out which is best for growing some runner beans. We can keep the results in a table and draw a bar chart to show our results clearly.'

A Look at the table of results on the left. A piece of information is missing. What is it? (Level 4)

Bar charts and line graphs

Bar charts and line graphs are used to show the relationship between two variables: the **independent variable** and the **dependent variable**. In a line graph or a bar chart the independent variable always goes along the *x*-axis. This is the axis that goes across the bottom of the graph.

There is an easy way to work out which variable is the independent variable and which is the dependent variable. Say to yourself, '**I** change the **I**ndependent variable and measure the dependent variable.' In the table on the left, the independent variable is the type of fertiliser.

B What is the dependent variable that Amber and her friends can measure? (Level 5)

The data from Amber, Ryan and Jasmine's experiment can be shown as a bar chart. Bar charts are used when the values of the independent variable are not related to or affected by each other. As the different types of fertiliser do not affect each other, Amber and her friends need to draw a bar chart.

Going for growth

When a seed germinates it uses its own stored food reserves to grow. After it has used up these reserves the seedling needs light to continue to grow. Becca decides to grow a plant for five weeks and give it light 24 hours a day. She then measures its height to see what its rate of growth is. Her results are shown in the table.

A line graph is used when you are comparing two variables that are both **continuous variables**. Becca plots the data in a line graph because the number of weeks and the heights of the plants are continuous.

Plant growth	
Week	**Height of plant (cm)**
0	1.5
1	2.1
2	2.7
3	3.2
4	4.0
5	4.6

To complete the line graph, Becca needs to draw a **line of best fit**. In science, this is a line that is drawn that shows the trend in the graph. You do not join the data points up 'dot to dot' as Becca has done. You draw a straight line or a smooth curve.

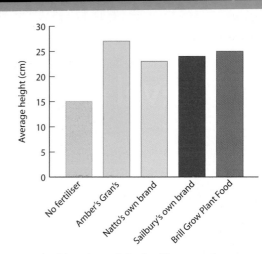

▲ A bar chart of the fertiliser experiment

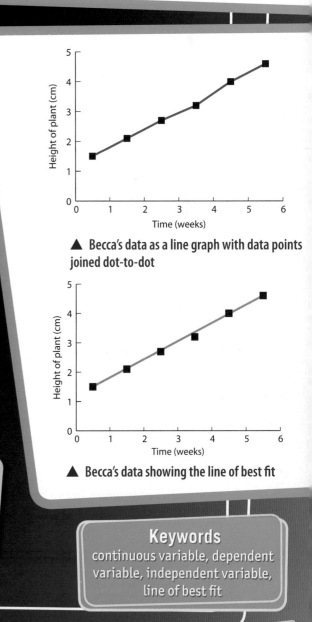

▲ Becca's data as a line graph with data points joined dot-to-dot

▲ Becca's data showing the line of best fit

C Explain what Becca's graph with a line of best fit shows about the relationship between the variables. (Level 6)

D Becca then repeats her experiment but this time keeps the plant in permanent darkness. Predict the difference between the growth rates of the plants in the two experiments. (Level 7)

Keywords

continuous variable, dependent variable, independent variable, line of best fit

Assess your progress

Level 4

1. In Dr Lind's experiment with the sailors on page 5, why was it important that they ate and drank the same, apart from the acid?

2. Ryan runs up a long steep hill. Explain how the muscles in his legs get energy from glucose, starting at the bottom of the hill and ending at the top.

3. Why do food manufacturers add additives to their products?

Level 5

4. The factor you change in an experiment is called the independent variable. Name the independent variable in Dr Lind's experiment on page 5.

5. Describe the journey of a piece of meat through the digestive system from your mouth to where the food particles get absorbed.

6. In Jasmine and Sam's experiment on page 13, why is it important that the two test tubes are exactly the same, apart from having mung beans in one of them?

7. Look at page 15 again. Why did Erasistratus's ideas have to wait for the invention of the microscope before they could be proved?

8. Ewan wants to investigate photosynthesis in water plants so he sets up an experiment. As the plants photosynthesise, bubbles of gas are given off and are collected in a boiling tube. Ewan shines different intensities of light onto the plants in the water. He counts the number of gas bubbles given off in one minute for each intensity of light. His results are shown in this line graph.

   Which two light intensities show the maximum number of bubbles being produced per minute?

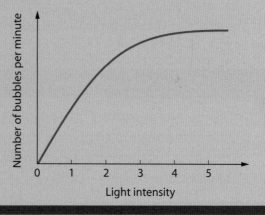

Level 6

9 Some doctors and parents have called for very overweight or very underweight children to be taken into care to prevent long-term damage being done to their bodies. Do you think that these children should be taken away from their parents? Explain your answer.

10 Why do you think the government has asked parents to reduce the number of food additives their children eat?

11 A farmer grows tomatoes in greenhouses. He cannot increase the amount of sunlight that comes through the windows. What can he do to increase the quantity of tomatoes that he grows?

12 Take a look at the London Underground map. It is one way of modelling what happens in the circulatory system. Explain the advantages and disadvantages of using it as a model.

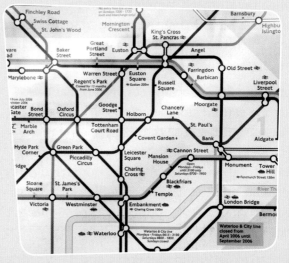

Level 7

13 Your body gets most of its energy from carbohydrates. Athletes get carbohydrates from starch in their diet. They can also take glucose, which is another form of carbohydrate, in tablet form. A starch molecule is made up of lots of glucose molecules joined together. In your digestive system, starch is broken down into glucose. Explain why an athlete can get energy more quickly by eating glucose rather than starch.

14 The gases that make up the Earth's atmosphere have varied over time. In the past 600 million years the percentage of oxygen in the air has varied from as low as 12% to as high as 35%. Imagine that you lived in a time when there was only 12% oxygen in the atmosphere. Explain how this would affect your respiratory system.

15 A company claims to have invented a chemical that, when added to cut flowers in a vase, will keep them fresh for up to three months. You intend to carry out an experiment to test the claim that cut flowers kept in water with the chemical added stay fresh for longer.
  a Which factor will be your independent variable and which will be your dependent variable?
  b Can you name at least one factor you should keep the same to ensure a fair test?
  c Make a prediction as to the outcome of your experiment.

In 1979 an Australian doctor called Robin Warren saw unusual spiral-shaped bacteria under his microscope when he was studying unhealthy stomach samples. He and his colleague, Barry Marshall, managed to grow these microbes from the stomach samples. They named them *Helicobacter pylori*.

Robin and Barry became convinced that this microbe caused stomach ulcers, like the one in the photo, because they kept finding the microbes in the unhealthy stomachs that they studied. Other doctors thought stomach ulcers were caused by stress, because they knew that people under stress produced lots of stomach acid.

Medical experts said that Robin and Barry's idea was 'preposterous'. They believed that bacteria could not survive in the acid, but Barry was so convinced that he tested it on himself. He drank a liquid containing the microbe and developed a stomach ulcer.

This discovery revolutionised the treatment of stomach ulcers. As a result of their research, Marshall and Warren were awarded a Nobel Prize in 2005.

Now try these

- Yeast is a microbe. It is used to make bread rise. What does yeast need to live, grow and reproduce?

- Some scientists use themselves in their medical experiments. Make a list of reasons why this may not be a good idea either for the individual or for scientific research.

- Alexander Fleming was the scientist who first observed that Penicillium mould killed bacteria, but it took many years until other scientists realised the possibility of using extracts of the mould as a medicine, and even longer until scientists produced the drug for use. Suggest why medical advances such as this take a long time.

Coming up in this Chapter ...

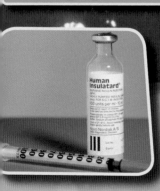

me people with diabetes cannot e without injections of insulin

Alexander Fleming discovered penicillin by accident in 1928

Vaccination has saved millions of lives worldwide

People can catch HIV by sharing infected needles

Learn about:

- how scientists discovered microbes
- how the classification of microbes has changed
- the different types of microbe
- how scientific ideas change over time

▲ Virus

▲ Fungus

▲ Bacterium

Microbes like the ones in the photos are far too small to be seen with the naked eye. It wasn't until the invention of the microscope in the seventeenth century that scientists discovered these tiny organisms.

Scientists now know that there are three main types of microbe. They are **bacteria**, **fungi** and **viruses**.

Classifying the new organisms

Before the seventeenth century, scientists had classified organisms as either plants or animals by looking at their features. Classifying tiny organisms was hard because it was difficult to see their features.

The invention of the microscope made it easier. In 1866, Ernst Haeckel added a third kingdom of microscopic organisms to the classification of living things.

 A Explain why Ernst Haeckel added a third kingdom to the classification system. (Level 4)

Modern classification of microbes

As more powerful microscopes were developed, scientists could see microbes in more detail, making the differences between different kinds of microbe clearer.

By 1969, scientists had made lots of observations of microbes with modern microscopes. This allowed them to suggest that there should be five kingdoms. These are plants, animals, single-celled organisms, bacteria and fungi.

Scientists often change their ideas as they make new findings. They are still developing new ways to classify microbes.

What are the features of microbes?

The table shows what bacteria, fungi and viruses are like.

Examples of microbes

Name	Structure	Example	Picture
Bacteria	Bacteria are single-celled organisms. They can be round balls, short sticks or spirals. Bacterial cells do not have a nucleus but they have a cell wall.	***E. coli*** is a bacterium which can cause food poisoning.	*E. coli*
Fungi	Fungi are larger than bacteria. Some fungi are small and round while other fungi are made of long threads. Fungi can be single-celled or have lots of cells.	**Yeast** is a tiny fungus and is used in brewing and baking.	Yeast
Viruses	Viruses are the smallest microbes. They are only about one millionth of a millimetre long. Many viruses are only visible with an electron microscope. They are not made of cells.	**HIV** is human immunodeficiency virus, which causes HIV/**AIDS**.	HIV virus

▲ Giant fungus in Kew Gardens

Not all fungi are microbes. One really giant fungus can be found in a shady corner of Kew Gardens near London. It is more than 170 cm across

B Suggest why fungi and bacteria were put into two different kingdoms. (Level 5)

Scientists have argued about whether viruses are living things or not, although most now say they are non-living. Viruses spring into action only when they get inside the cells of another living thing. Even bacteria can be invaded by a virus.

C Explain why scientists disagree about the classification of viruses as living things when they are in agreement about bacteria and fungi. (Level 6)

D Discuss why some fungi are microscopic and others are not. (Level 6)

Early microscopes, such as those developed in the seventeenth century by Leeuwenhoek and Hooke, showed tiny organisms for the first time. Using modern microscopes, scientists can now identify them as bacteria or viruses.

E List *three* key points used by scientists in classifying a microbe as either a bacteria or a virus. (Level 7)

Interesting fact

One litre of seawater from the deep Pacific or Atlantic oceans can contain 20,000 different types of bacteria.

Keywords

AIDS, bacteria, *E. coli*, fungus, HIV, microbe, virus, yeast

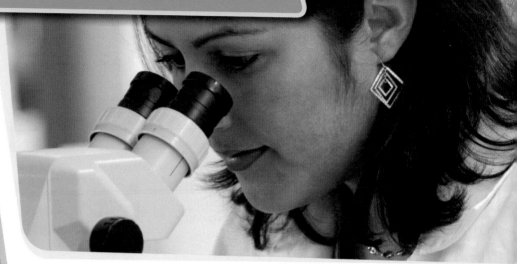

Learn about:

- how some microbes are useful
- how some scientific breakthroughs are partly luck and partly good science
- how scientists, usually working in teams, build on the work of other scientists to make new discoveries

▲ Lottie is a scientist and a diabetic

Lottie is a scientist working at Genentech in San Francisco, California. She is involved in producing human **insulin**. She is also a **diabetic** so she understands how important this is.

We all need insulin to control the level of sugar in our blood. Insulin is made in an organ called the **pancreas**. Diabetics do not produce insulin for themselves and so they have to inject it. Without insulin they would die.

In 1978, the Genentech laboratory working with the City of Hope National Medical Centre in the US successfully produced human insulin using bacteria. Scientists managed to put the human **gene** for making insulin into bacteria. The bacteria then act as a 'factory', producing insulin.

> **A** (i) Why do diabetics need to be given insulin? (ii) Suggest where insulin came from before scientists managed to produce it using bacteria. (Level 4)

▲ Alexander Fleming made a scientific breakthrough by chance

Penicillin

In 1928, a scientist called Alexander Fleming was growing bacteria on an **agar plate**. Agar is a special type of jelly which scientists use to grow microbes. He accidentally left the agar plate on his laboratory desk while he went away on holiday. During his holiday a **mould**, which is a type of fungus, landed on the dish.

When Fleming returned he noticed that the area around the mould was clear of bacteria. He realised that the mould was producing an antibiotic, which he called **penicillin** after the Penicillium mould that produced it.

B Fleming noticed that the area around the mould was clear of bacteria. (i) What did this observation suggest to Fleming? (ii) What did other scientists go on to do later, based on Fleming's discovery? (Level 5)

Teamwork in science

Ten years later, a scientist called Howard Florey was working with a team of scientists at Oxford University. Ernst Chain, a member of the team, saw an account of Fleming's work in a medical journal and the group started to experiment with penicillin.

They each concentrated on what they were good at and worked weekends to complete their results and carry out tests with the new drug. Teams of scientists often work together today but it was not common at that time.

By 1945 penicillin was available in small amounts and was used to treat soldiers who had been injured in battle during the Second World War.

C Why wasn't penicillin available to the general public when it was given to injured soldiers? (Level 6)

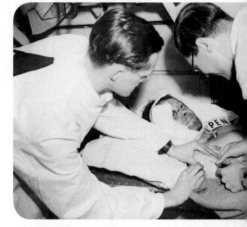
▲ Penicillin – a life saver

Foul Fact

The first man treated with penicillin had blood poisoning. The penicillin started to cure it. Each night his urine was collected and 'distilled' to get the penicillin back to use the next day. Unfortunately, they still ran out of penicillin and he died.

More uses for microbes

Since ancient times we have used the yeast fungus to produce wine, beer and bread. Moulds can be added to cheese to make blue cheese.

Bacteria are used in making cheese and yoghurt. They are also used in sewage works to break down sewage. They are also able to break down the dead bodies of animals and plants.

Bacteria can divide very quickly when conditions are warm and moist. They can grow and divide into two every 20 minutes.

> We have 'friendly' bacteria living in our gut. They help us to digest our food.

▲ Quorn, which is made from fungi, is often eaten by vegetarians to replace meat in their meals

D Professor Germ says: 'One single bacterium can become more than 8 million cells in less than 24 hours!' Is he exaggerating? Discuss his statement. (Level 7)

Keywords
agar plate, diabetic, gene, insulin, mould, pancreas, penicillin

2.4 Death to microbes

Learn about:

- how microbes can cause disease
- how microbes get into your body and how your body stops them
- how microbes can be killed

▲ Hospital wards need to be cleaned thoroughly to get rid of bacteria

Not all microbes are useful. Some can cause dangerous diseases or infections if they get inside our bodies. The MRSA infection found in hospitals is caused by bacteria. These bacteria are difficult to destroy and can cause serious infections and death in patients.

Other microbes are just as deadly. In 1918, at the end of the First World War, the influenza virus killed 21 million people worldwide. You can see in the table some more examples of microbes and the illnesses they cause.

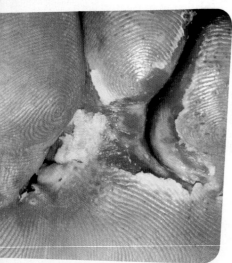

▲ Athlete's foot

Microbes and illness	
Type of microbe	**Illnesses caused**
bacteria	meningitis, food poisoning, tuberculosis, typhoid, whooping cough, syphilis
viruses	colds, flu, tetanus, measles, chicken pox
fungi	athlete's foot, thrush

A Look at the table. What type of microbe causes: (i) thrush (ii) typhoid (iii) measles? (Level 4)

Foul Fact

Ebola is one of the most deadly viruses and at the moment there is no cure for it. It causes vomiting, diarrhoea and internal bleeding. It kills up to 90% of its victims.

Microbe invasion

Microbes can get into your body in lots of different ways:

- through cuts in your skin
- in the food you eat
- in the water you drink
- in the air you breathe
- through your eyes

But microbes don't have it all their own way. Your body has ways of stopping them.

B Most of the time our skin prevents microbes from entering the body. If you have a bad cut, the bleeding washes the cut and helps to clean it. What happens next to a cut to stop microbes from getting into the body? (Level 5)

C Your respiratory system is lined with tiny hairs and has cells which produce a sticky mucus. Explain how this helps to prevent microbes from entering your body. (Level 6)

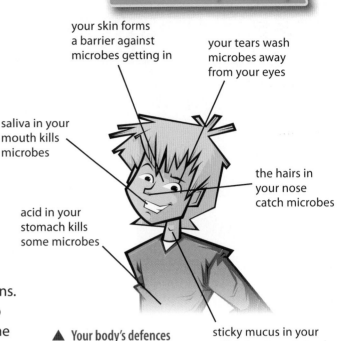

your skin forms a barrier against microbes getting in

your tears wash microbes away from your eyes

saliva in your mouth kills microbes

the hairs in your nose catch microbes

acid in your stomach kills some microbes

▲ Your body's defences

sticky mucus in your windpipe traps microbes

Killing microbes

Another way of reducing the chance of microbes entering our bodies is to use **antiseptics** and **disinfectants**. We use antiseptics to stop bacteria getting into wounds, and disinfectants to kill microbes on floors and toilets.

For centuries, wounds often became infected after operations. Doctors used to apply tar to amputated arms or legs to stop this happening. In 1867, a doctor called Joseph Lister had the idea that microbes caused wounds to become infected. He discovered that the tar contained **carbolic acid** which killed bacteria around the wound.

This discovery led to doctors using carbolic acid sprays during operations. Now surgeons scrub their hands and arms with antiseptics before they carry out an operation. The operating theatre is also kept clean with disinfectants.

D In what two ways can putting tar on a wound prevent it from becoming infected? (Level 6)

▼ Antiseptics are used to kill bacteria outside our bodies

Antibiotics

You have already seen how Alexander Fleming discovered penicillin. Penicillin is a type of medicine called an **antibiotic**. Antibiotics kill bacteria. The discovery of penicillin led to lots of other antibiotics being developed.

Antibiotics do not kill viruses. This is why a doctor may prescribe antibiotics for a sore throat, which is usually a bacterial infection, but not for the flu, which is caused by a virus.

When you take antibiotics, it is very important that you finish the treatment. If you do not, then some bacteria might survive and begin to reproduce. These bacteria can become resistant to antibiotics. This means they are not killed.

E Some of the bacteria that cause infections in hospitals are called 'super-bugs'. Suggest why they are given this name. (Level 7)

Keywords
antibiotic, antiseptic, carbolic acid, disinfectant

2.5 Becoming immune

Learn about:
- how your body fights infection
- what vaccination is and how it works
- how vaccines were developed

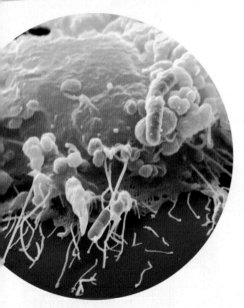

▲ A white blood cell 'eating' a bacterium

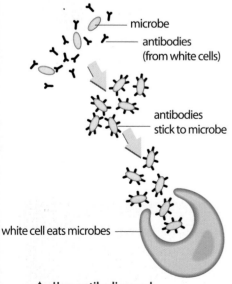

microbe

antibodies (from white cells)

antibodies stick to microbe

white cell eats microbes

▲ How antibodies work

▲ Lots of children are vaccinated against measles, mumps and rubella

Measles kills about a million children worldwide each year. It is caused by a virus. It starts off like a cold and then you develop a rash and can have vomiting and diarrhoea. There can be fatal complications so children in the UK are **vaccinated** with the measles, mumps and rubella **(MMR) vaccine**.

Hunt and destroy

When disease-causing microbes get into your body, special cells in your blood called **white blood cells** get to work. They form part of your **immune system** which protects you from disease.

White blood cells can fight microbes in different ways:

- They can 'eat' microbes and destroy them.
- They can produce chemicals called **antibodies**. These antibodies attach themselves to the outside of microbes. Antibodies either make the microbes stick together (which makes it easier for white blood cells to surround them), or destroy the microbes directly.

White blood cells produce different antibodies to fight different microbes. If your body has already met a microbe, then if the invader returns your immune system can quickly produce the right antibodies to fight it off. Scientists call this being **immune** to a disease.

A Describe the ways in which white blood cells destroy invading microbes. (Level 4)

How vaccination works

When you are vaccinated against a disease you are injected with dead or inactive microbes. The microbes do not make you ill, although you can sometimes have mild symptoms. Your body develops antibodies. If the active microbes ever get into your body you can quickly produce antibodies against them. This is called **active immunity**. You can also be injected with ready-made antibodies, which is called **passive immunity**.

> ## Interesting fact
>
> Newborn babies receive antibodies in breast milk. This is one reason why doctors tell mothers that 'breast is best'.

B Explain the difference between active immunity and passive immunity. (Level 5)

Smallpox

For hundreds of years smallpox was a deadly disease. In Turkey, in the early eighteenth century, doctors used to give people pus from smallpox sores which contained live microbes. The idea was that the people would get a mild form of the disease and when they recovered they would be immune. But sometimes this went wrong and the person died.

In 1796, a doctor called Edward Jenner noticed that milkmaids did not get smallpox. But they did get a weaker form of the disease called cowpox. Jenner scratched some pus from a cowpox sore into the skin of a boy called James Phipps. The boy developed cowpox but soon recovered. Later, Jenner infected James with smallpox, but James was now immune to it and did not develop the disease. This was the first vaccination against smallpox.

Nowadays, there are vaccines for lots of different diseases and most of them contain a weak form of the disease.

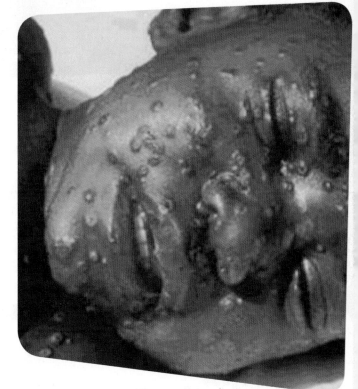

▲ Smallpox causes sores full of pus to develop all over the body

C The term 'vaccination' comes from the Latin word for cowpox which is 'Vaccinia'. Edward Jenner introduced this term to describe his procedure. The term is still used today. Explain why it was a good term to use. (Level 6)

D The investigation that Jenner carried out was very dangerous, although it led to the discovery of vaccination and eventually saved millions of lives. Imagine that you are each of the characters below and write a statement explaining your opinion of the experiment: (i) Edward Jenner (ii) James Phipps (iii) A doctor who thinks Jenner's theory is wrong. (Level 7)

> ## Keywords
>
> active immunity, antibody, immune, immune system, MMR vaccine, passive immunity, vaccinate, white blood cell

2.6 Bird flu – a worldwide threat

Learn about:

- how scientists have discovered that bird flu started in the Far East and has spread around the world
- how studying patterns of spread may help scientists to control the disease

Three swans found dead at Dorset swannery, Jan 11 2008

▲ The three dead mute swans had the H5N1 strain of bird flu

Influenza (flu) can be a dangerous disease. In the early 1900s millions of people around the world died from it. Flu is caused by a virus. There are different flu viruses which affect different animals.

There is a very dangerous flu virus called H5N1 which causes flu in birds such as turkeys, chickens and swans. Since the late 1990s scientists have seen this disease spread across the world.

Many birds migrate long distances to warmer climates in winter. They can spread the disease on their journey. The Dorset swans had a similar disease to some other swans which died in the Czech Republic earlier in the year. Ornithologists (bird experts) say that mute swans do not often migrate so the swans in Dorset may have picked up the disease from other passing infected birds.

▼ Areas with bird flu in 2004

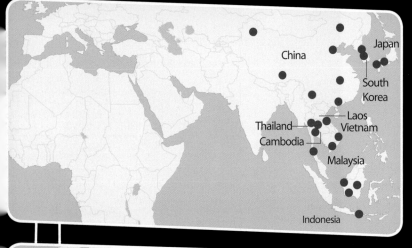

▲ Areas with bird flu in 2007

The risk to humans

Scientists are worried about the H5N1 virus because humans can catch from infected birds. People who live near birds or work closely with them are at particular risk. Scientists are worried that this virus might change into a form which can be passed from person to person and kill millions of people. Some doctors believe that some cases have been passed from human to human already. If the bird flu virus does change scientists estimate that 2–50 million people worldwide could die.

Foul Fact

Birds pass the flu virus on through their faeces which dry out into dust. This dust can then be breathed in by other birds or humans.

A Why are scientists particularly worried about the H5N1 strain of bird flu? (Level 4)

B People who keep poultry in areas that migrating birds fly over have been told to keep their poultry under cover, especially when wild birds are migrating. How might this reduce the spread of bird flu? (Level 5)

Keeping track of the spread

Scientists rely on farmers, bird watchers and the general public to report dead birds. They can then arrange to find out if the birds did die of bird flu. Knowing how the disease might spread allows scientists to plan ahead, to act quickly and to have vaccines available in the right place. Where bird flu is identified, whole flocks of farm birds may have to be destroyed by vets. Birds are killed over the whole of an area surrounding the outbreak and birds cannot be moved in or out of that area to limit the spread.

C During a bird flu outbreak farmers are banned from moving farm birds in and out of the affected area. Birds like racing pigeons may also be banned from leaving their lofts and markets selling live birds may be closed. Why are these actions very important in the control of the disease? (Level 6)

▼ Recorded incidents of bird flu

Glasgow

Belfast

Manchester

Birmingham

Norwich

London

2 March 2006
Whooper swan in Fife dies of bird flu. It was a visitor to Britain

3 April 2006
Chickens test positive for bird flu on a farm in Norfolk. 35,000 birds are slaughtered

4 February 2007
159,000 turkeys are slaughtered in Suffolk after some are discovered to have the disease

5 November 2007
Birds slaughtered at several farms in Suffolk because of bird flu

6 January 2007
Dead swans found in Dorset

1 October 2005
Imported parrots and finches in quarantine in Essex die of bird flu

D The UK's chief vet has asked farmers, poultry keepers and the general public to keep a close look out for signs of bird flu. (i) Why is it important that all possible cases are identified and recorded? (ii) Why are cases in other countries important in the study of the disease? (iii) Why is the strain of bird flu important? (Level 7)

Assess your progress

Level 4

1   The classification of microbes has changed several times since they were first recognised in the seventeenth century. How have modern microscopes helped scientists to finally agree on a way of classifying them?

2   Why should scientists at Genentech use very strict safety precautions when they are working with bacteria?

3   Your eyes provide a way for microbes to enter your body. What reduces the chances of this happening?

4   Babies do not receive their first childhood vaccinations until they are 2 months old. What can help to keep them healthy before this?

5   Scientists need early warning about possible cases of bird flu. Who might be of help to them in getting this information?

Level 5

6   Look at the diagrams of a bacterium, a virus and a fungus. What are the similarities and differences between each one and a typical animal cell?

7   Tyrone has been studying the microbe yeast in his science lesson. His mother makes her own bread at home but has been having a problem getting it to rise. Tyrone tells her that she should put the yeast, water and sugar mixture in the warm airing cupboard for 20 minutes. Is this good advice? Explain his reasoning.

8   a Identify three diseases which can be cured by giving the patient antibiotics.

   b Explain why antibiotics are not given to a patient with chicken pox.

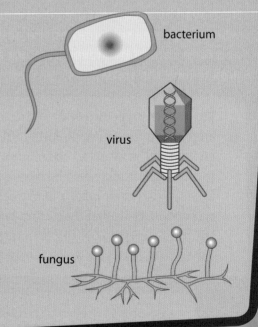

bacterium

virus

fungus

Level 6

9 Lance's class has been learning about microbes. He knows that viruses are the smallest of the three types. To help him understand just how small they are, his teacher has asked him to find out approximately how many virus particles would fit across the 1 mm space on his ruler. Use your knowledge of viruses to help him solve this problem.

10 Suggest how 'friendly bacteria' help us to digest our food.

11 Look at Jenner's experiment on James Phipps on page 31. It was extremely risky. Explain why Jenner would not be allowed to carry out his experiment today.

12 During the bird flu outbreak in Suffolk in February 2007, a vet who was involved in testing the birds was taken ill. Other people involved in the clean-up were offered medicines that kill viruses.
   a Why were doctors worried about the vet?
   b Why did they give the cleaning team medicines that kill viruses?

Level 7

13 Explain why a virus cannot be classified as a typical plant or animal cell.

14 'Germaway' disinfectant products are designed to kill microbes to reduce the chances of infection. The makers of 'Germaway' spray say that it kills 99% of microbes in 30 seconds. Describe in outline how a scientist could test this statement.

15 Look at the graph. It shows the number of cases of measles between 1944 and 2000 in the USA. Suggest what led to the small fall in measles cases before the vaccine was introduced. Why do you think there was a rise in the number of cases in the late 1980s?

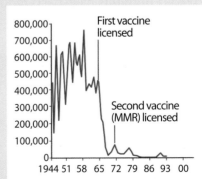

16 The first cases of bird flu recorded in the UK were in October 2005. These occurred in quarantined birds.
   a During a period of quarantine, birds from one area are kept separated from others. Why is this a good idea?
   b Could quarantine stop bird flu altogether in the UK?
   c If you were a government adviser how would you decide on the length of the quarantine period?

Yellowstone National Park in the USA covers 8987 km^2 of lakes, canyons, rivers and mountain ranges. It is home to hundreds of species of animals and plants. Wolves had always lived in the area but they were a problem to ranchers because they ate their livestock.

Government 'bounty hunters' wiped the wolves out by the 1920s. Scientists noticed that the loss of the wolves had affected many animals and plants in the park. Aspen and cottonwood trees had been lost and some birds, insects, fish and other plants had also suffered.

Conservationists realised that the wolves kept the numbers of grazing animals such as elk under control. Once the wolves had gone there were more elk to eat the tree saplings. Without the trees, rivers washed away more of the soil and beavers could not build dams. Many other species were affected.

Conservationists wanted to reintroduce the wolves. Ranchers were afraid for their herds. It was agreed that ranchers would be paid for any animals they lost and in 1995, 160 wolves returned. Today the trees are growing back because the elk numbers have been reduced by the return of their natural predator.

Now try these

- Draw a food chain linking the aspen tree, wolves and elks.

- Some ranchers went to court to try to prevent the Yellowstone wolf project. Explain why the ranchers were unhappy about the reintroduction of wolves.

- Yellowstone Park is an example of a national park where the animals and plants are conserved. There are areas like this throughout the world. What do we mean by 'conservation' and why is it important to have conservation areas of all sizes from small patches in our gardens to enormous jungle areas in countries such as Africa?

Coming up in this Chapter ...

Chimps learn how to use tools

Coral reefs form large ecosystems around the world

Predators like owls keep animal populations in check

Ecologists work outdoors studying the environment

▲ Cereals for breakfast

Andrea lives on a farm. A barn owl lives in one of the barns and Andrea sometimes sees the owl returning home in the evening with a harvest mouse that it has caught. Harvest mice feed on the wheat that grows in the nearby fields.

Pyramids of numbers

A food chain shows how materials and energy flow from plants to animals according to their feeding relationships. Scientists use a model called a **pyramid of numbers** to represent the numbers of these organisms at each level in the food chain.

The diagram below shows the pyramid of numbers for the wheat → mice → owl food chain. The wide base shows at a glance that many ears of wheat are eaten by a smaller number of mice. The top layer represents only one barn owl.

> Pyramids of numbers are drawn so that the size of each layer represents the numbers of organisms present. We say that they are drawn 'to scale'.

A   What is shown by a pyramid of numbers? (Level 4)

B   Explain why pyramids of numbers should be drawn to scale. (Level 5)

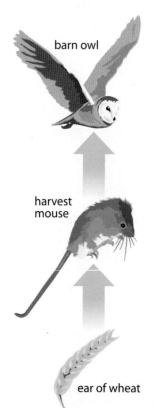

▲ A food chain for wheat, mice and owl

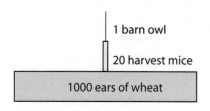

| 1 barn owl |
| 20 harvest mice |
| 1000 ears of wheat |

▲ A pyramid of numbers

Energy flow

There are usually fewer and fewer consumers as you go up a food chain. Why is this? One explanation is that organisms higher up a food chain are usually larger than the organisms they feed on. An owl needs lots of mice to survive.

But at each stage of feeding, energy is also 'lost' to the environment. Energy is stored in the wheat. A mouse eats the wheat and the energy is transferred to the mouse. But the mouse changes some of the energy into movement and heat. So when the owl eats the mouse, only some of the energy from the wheat is transferred into the owl.

C Farmers often spray their wheat with chemicals which kill the insect pests that eat it. Mice eat the wheat without any problems, but top predators like owls can be badly affected by the chemical. Suggest why this is the case. (Level 5)

▲ One owl will eat lots of mice

Pyramids that aren't pyramids

Sometimes a pyramid of numbers is not a pyramid at all! Look at the pyramid of numbers for this garden food chain: rose tree → greenflies → blue tit.

This pyramid of numbers is an odd shape. It looks as though there are too many greenflies to live on one rose tree. The pyramid is an odd shape because the rose tree is so large in mass compared to the greenfly – one rose tree can feed lots of greenflies.

Scientists use **pyramids of biomass** to get around this problem. They show the total amount of mass of the organisms at each level of a food chain.

D Explain why the pyramid of numbers model does not work in all cases. (Level 6)

All change

Conditions in the environment change with the seasons and over longer periods of time. Factors such as climate change or disease can affect the numbers of organisms in the food chain.

E What might cause the numbers of small mammals in an area to: (i) decrease (ii) increase? Many farmers are keen to help conserve the environment. (iii) What can they do to keep small mammal numbers as high as possible so that the owls survive? (Level 7)

▼ Tawny owls have to compete for food with other owls

A pair of tawny owls has moved into the area near Andrea's barn. They eat small mammals such as mice and voles. The owls **compete** for prey with each other and with birds like kestrels. In a good year there may be enough for everyone, but if the numbers of small mammals fall some birds may have to move to other areas. In times of extreme shortage some birds may die.

Science at work

Scientists are trying to develop chemical-free methods of pest control. For example, ladybirds can be introduced into greenhouses to control greenflies.

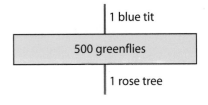

▲ Pyramid of biomass for garden food chain

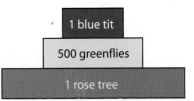

▲ Pyramid of numbers for garden food chain

Keywords
compete, pyramid of biomass, pyramid of numbers

39

3.3 Relying on each other

Learn about:

- how and why populations change
- how food webs can help scientists to predict changes in a population

The planet Zorb is home to a vast number of animals and plants unlike anything we see on Earth. But, like the animals on Earth, the flora and fauna on Zorb rely on each other. Gronks are small Zorbian creatures that only emerge to feed in the early hours of the morning before dawn. They get water from the early morning dew and feed on the lush grass and the seeds of the Blue Toppa plant.

Drangs live in underground burrows, leaving their holes to prey mainly on Gronks. The colourful Zooby birds also prey on Gronks although they prefer to feed on other creatures when they can.

▲ Zooby birds compete with each other for food

 A Draw a food web for grass, Blue Toppa seeds, Zooby birds, Drangs and Gronks. (Level 4)

Competing to live

The Gronks, Drangs and Zooby birds exist together in a **habitat**. Scientists say that different species that exist together like this form a **community**. Scientists call the number of organisms of a particular species living in a habitat a **population**. There is **competition** between the organisms in a habitat.

The size of any population depends on competition between the organisms for food, water and space. It also depends on how many of them are eaten by predators. The different species in a habitat are all **interdependent**.

The Gronks' tale

Two Gronks have built their nest in a deserted, tumble-down shelter. Around the shelter there is plenty of grass and the Blue Toppa plants are full of seeds. There is lots for them to eat and plenty of places for them to hide from their predators. In this ideal habitat the Gronk population grows to 95. The Gronks are competing with each other for:

- food
- clean water
- space
- a mate.

But after some time the population begins to go down. The table shows how the population of Gronks changes.

Changes in Gronk population	
Time (weeks)	Number of Gronks
0	2
5	14
10	35
15	58
20	79
25	95
30	95
35	90
40	87

B (i) Draw a line graph of the data in the table. (ii) Label the graph to show when the population growth was quickest and when the number of Gronks being born was equal to the number of Gronks dying. (Level 5)

C Suggest what factors caused the Gronk population to go down. (Level 6)

A Zooby bird has discovered the Gronks living in the shelter. There are so many Gronks that they become the Zooby birds' main source of food. More and more Zooby birds come to feed on the Gronks in the shelter.

D Use the food web you drew in question **A** to predict what will happen to the Zooby birds when the Gronk population goes down. (Level 7)

A suspicious death

The size of a population can also depend on how many of the organisms die from disease or are poisoned by weedkillers or pesticides. On planet Zorb, Mindal's father sprays weedkiller on his garden and the spray accidentally blows onto the land surrounding his garden.

Shortly after, Mindal finds a dead Zooby bird near the house. A vet from the Zorb Society for the Protection of Birds investigates and shows that the Zooby bird has been poisoned by the weedkiller.

▲ What killed this Zooby bird?

E Use your knowledge of pyramids of numbers to explain how the Zooby bird received a large enough dose of the weedkiller to kill it. (Level 7)

Keywords
community, competition, habitat, interdependent, population

▲ Ecologists can work around the world as well as close to home

Ecologists are scientists who are interested in how living things interact with their environment. Through investigations and observations they find clues to help solve environmental problems such as habitat damage, species extinction and climate change. They often work outside as well as in their laboratories.

A What are ecologists especially interested in? (Level 4)

Eco detective

In 1975 a group of mothers in Lyme, Connecticut in the USA realised that their children all had the same illness. Detective work showed that it was caused by bacteria which were spread by ticks – small parasites (like fleas) carried by deer, sheep and other mammals. People can pick up the ticks when they walk in woodland or moorland.

Some people wanted to kill the deer, but ecologists knew that this alone would not necessarily prevent the disease. The ticks are carried by other animals too and can live in the grass for long periods. This disease was called Lyme disease after the place where it was identified. You can also get Lyme disease in the UK.

▲ Ticks can spread the bacteria that give you Lyme disease

Problems with ecosystems

There are many different **ecosystems** on Earth and they all include different habitats and varieties of living things. Ecosystems on Earth include tropical rainforest, desert, grassland and ocean.

Ecologists are very concerned about many ecosystems, but one part of the ocean ecosystem is causing a lot of concern – the Great Barrier Reef off the coast of Australia. It is bigger than the whole of Italy and is made from small animals called **coral** which are related to jellyfish.

This coral reef is frequently attacked by the crown of thorns starfish which is almost the only animal able to feed on the coral. These starfish are not a threat when the numbers are low, but when the population rises they can cause enormous damage.

Ecologists have studied the outbreaks of starfish that have occurred over the last 40 years. These have become more frequent and this is thought to be due to human activity.

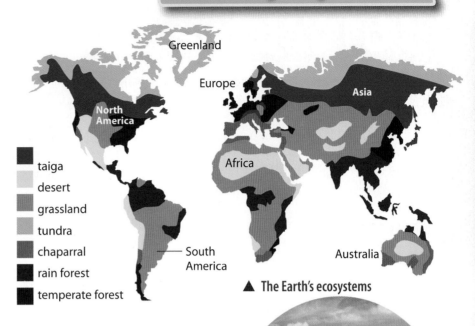

- taiga
- desert
- grassland
- tundra
- chaparral
- rain forest
- temperate forest

▲ The Earth's ecosystems

B Particularly important or unique areas on Earth can be declared World Heritage Sites to preserve them. Why is this necessary? (Level 5)

C The Great Barrier Reef is the world's largest World Heritage Site. (i) How might the reef's status as a World Heritage Site help ecologists to preserve it? (ii) How will discovering the reasons for starfish outbreaks help to preserve the Great Barrier Reef? (Level 6)

▲ The Great Barrier Reef is being attacked by the crown of thorns starfish

Reef food webs

Look at the food web for a coral reef. The reef food web is complicated, with many different animals and plants involved, so the diagram only shows part of the food web.

If the numbers of organisms in this part of the food web change, there will be changes elsewhere. Humans have caused changes to numbers of organisms by polluting the oceans with sewage and chemicals and by over-fishing of reef-living creatures such as lobsters, sharks and shellfish.

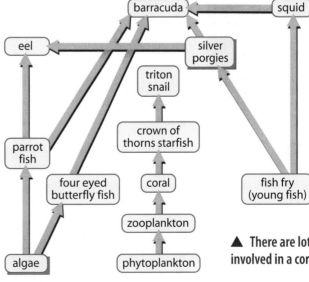

barracuda · squid · eel · silver porgies · triton snail · crown of thorns starfish · parrot fish · four eyed butterfly fish · coral · fish fry (young fish) · zooplankton · algae · phytoplankton

▲ There are lots of organisms involved in a coral reef food web

D In some areas divers have removed large numbers of starfish. What effect might this have on: (i) the numbers of triton snails (ii) the growth of the coral? (Level 7)

Keywords
coral, ecologist, ecosystem

3.5 You live and learn

Learn about:

- what influences an animal's behaviour
- how an animal's behaviour can be changed
- what psychologists study

▶ A learning experience

▲ Practice makes perfect

Although birds and mammals often look after their offspring, very few animals actually teach their offspring skills that help them to survive.

Cheetah mothers teach their cubs to hunt. They capture gazelles which they put in front of the cubs. Every time the gazelle gets away the mother cheetah brings it back. The cubs' instinct is to chase, and in this way they improve their hunting skills which increases their chances of survival.

Human beings are different from other animals because they teach their children a vast number of skills over a long period.

A How do parent birds care for their offspring? (Level 4)

Do as I do

It is difficult to be sure how young animals, other than humans, learn, but many scientists think that it is mainly through trial and error or through observing their parents. Young birds quickly learn to recognise their mother and soon follow her around. This means they can learn from her behaviour.

A human baby may recognise their mother's voice at birth because they were aware of it while still in the womb. It takes a little longer to recognise her face because babies can't focus their eyes immediately after birth.

▲ Do chimpanzees learn to use tools by watching others in the troop?

Interesting fact

Young shrews learn what to eat by licking their mother's mouth to learn what she eats.

B Why is it an advantage to be able to recognise her voice? (Level 5)

C (i) Why is it not possible to know exactly how animals other than humans learn? (ii) How can scientists try to find out? (Level 6)

Changing behaviour

Animals need to be able to change their behaviour when conditions in their environment change. If they don't do this they may die. They need to recognise a suitable mate so that the species is kept going, and they need to be able to spot danger and to recognise suitable foods.

Even simple animals like butterflies are known to learn by experience. They prefer feeding from flowers of a particular colour, but they can change their preference. This is an advantage if those coloured flowers are in short supply. Without the ability to learn and change their behaviour the butterflies would die.

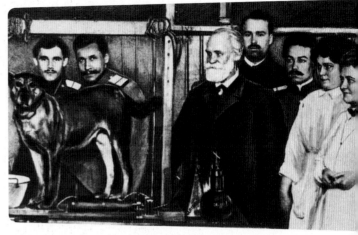

▲ Pavlov experimented on dogs

Pavlov's dogs

Scientists called **psychologists** are interested in how humans and animals learn and behave. Ivan Pavlov was a famous scientist born in Russia in 1894 who studied the behaviour of dogs.

Pavlov noticed that when his dogs were given food they produced saliva. This helped them start digesting their food. Pavlov did an experiment. He started to ring a buzzer when he gave the dogs their food.

He found that if he rang the buzzer the dogs produced saliva even when there was no food. He had linked what he called an **unconditioned stimulus** (the food) to a **conditioned stimulus** (the buzzer) through training which he called **conditioning**. This was an important discovery about the way animals learn and can be trained.

At one time, animals such as lions, elephants and bears were trained to do circus tricks. Many people went to the circus to watch them. Some people did not believe that this was the right way to treat animals and gradually it has stopped, although in some countries animals are still trained to perform.

> **D** Suggest why many people object to the training of wild animals. (Level 6)

Army dog Sadie awarded the animal VC

Dogs are often used by the Army in wartime. British army dog Sadie was awarded a medal for her work in Afghanistan as a search dog for explosives. This work saves many lives. Sadie learned through training how to find the scent of explosives and how to let her handler know that she had found them.

Using instincts

Many animals, such as dogs, have instinctive behaviours which can be changed by training so that they can be useful to humans.

> **E** (i) What inborn abilities do dogs like Sadie have that make them good at discovering explosives? (ii) Sadie's handler, Lance Corporal Karen Yardley, is an experienced soldier. Why can she not find the explosives as efficiently as Sadie? (Level 7)

> **Keywords**
> conditioning, conditioned stimulus, psychologist, unconditioned stimulus

3.6 The great badger debate

Learn about:

- how scientific research can solve problems
- how evidence can be inconclusive
- how scientists' decisions affect people

▲ Are badgers dangerous?

My name is George and I work for the Badger Trust. We provide expert advice on badger issues helping to identify and protect the setts where they live. We believe that TB is not spread by badgers but is spread by farmers moving cattle around the country to farms and market.

My name is Claire and I'm a member of the National Farmers' Union. Many farmers keep cattle and TB is a problem for them. If a cow in their herd catches TB they cannot sell the milk and the cow will have to be destroyed. Humans can catch TB from milk if it has not been pasteurized. We think that badgers do spread TB to cattle.

Tuberculosis (TB) is a serious disease caused by a bacterium. It was once a big problem in this country causing serious illness and many deaths.

Today we can vaccinate people against it and we have some antibiotics which we can use to treat it. However, the bacteria that cause it are becoming resistant to these antibiotics and some doctors are worried that tuberculosis may become a big problem again.

A   Describe how tuberculosis can be prevented and how it can sometimes be treated. (Level 4)

Badgers on trial

Cattle and badgers are two other species that can suffer from TB. For a long time some people have believed that badgers pass TB onto cattle but others have disagreed.

In 1998, a 5-year investigation was started to find the truth by collecting evidence. This involved killing or **culling** badgers in a particular area to see whether the numbers of cattle with TB dropped. Defra is the government department for the environment and rural affairs. It was in charge of the scientific trial. The trial was not easy to carry out. Lots of people objected to it and some people tried to sabotage it.

B   Suggest why some people were against the experiment to find out if badgers were responsible for spreading tuberculosis. (Level 4)

C Suggest why it is important to know if badgers are spreading tuberculosis. (Level 5)

▲ Any badgers killed in road traffic accidents were also tested for TB

Collecting the data

When the trial was planned, there were 300 000 badgers in the UK. The trial killed 11 000 of them in 30 areas of the country where lots of cows catch TB. These are called high infection areas. Badgers are protected under the 1992 Protection of Badgers Act and killing them required a special licence.

Scientists divided the high infection areas into three smaller areas. In one they killed as many badgers as possible. In another they killed no badgers, but checked to see if there were some badgers living there. In the third they killed badgers on and around farms where there were definite cases of TB.

They wanted to compare the effects of these measures on the number of cases of TB in cows. They compared the numbers of cases of TB in cattle which showed up in the different smaller areas studied. To avoid reducing badger numbers too much they did not kill badgers from February to April to protect females with young. Badgers were trapped using cages and were humanely destroyed.

D (i) Why were badgers found dead as a result of road accidents tested for TB? (ii) How might the information gained in this way help scientists plan a wider investigation involving deliberately culling badgers? (Level 6)

Do badgers spread TB?

The results did not prove that badgers definitely spread TB. In fact the number of cases of TB in cattle has increased despite the badger cull. This is why scientists still believe that badgers do contribute to the spread of TB. Scientists think that this may be due to badgers wandering further in areas where they are being killed and spreading TB even more.

Cases of TB detected in badgers killed in road accidents in the South West between 1972 and 1998			Devon	Cornwall	Somerset
1972-1995	Examined		1029	2158	900
	TB positive		25	67	3
	% positive		2.4	3.1	0.3
1996	Examined		39	133	25
	TB positive		6	8	3
	% positive		15.4	6.0	12.0
1997	Examined		61	139	41
	TB positive		3	5	1
	% positive		4.9	3.6	2.4
1998	Examined		81	165	43
	TB positive		4	10	6
	% positive		4.9	6.1	14.0

E (i) How many badgers were examined in Cornwall during the period of the study? (ii) Describe how the number of badgers in Devon found to be carrying TB changed over the period of the study. (Level 7)

Keywords
cull, tuberculosis (TB)

Assess your progress

1   A biologist is interested in the feeding relationships between organisms living around a tree. On a field trip he sees caterpillars on the bark, a woodpecker on the trunk and bats flying around. He notices a fox a short distance away and a squirrel is eating the nuts from the branches. Draw a possible food chain from his observations.

2   On Earth, foxes feed on rabbits. What would happen to the size of the rabbit population if the fox population fell?

3   Tourists enjoy visiting the Great Barrier Reef. What are the advantages and disadvantages of tourism for reefs?

4   Jamie is starting to get his puppy to sit at the kerb when they cross the road. Every time the puppy gets this right he rewards him with a small treat. How will this help train the puppy?

5   Sonya draws a pyramid of numbers for the following food chain:
    oak tree ⟶ caterpillars ⟶ sparrow
    Why is it not pyramid shaped?

6   Raj is investigating the creatures living in his garden. As part of his project Raj records his observations about the number of woodlice under a pot in his garden. He notes that the population has increased. What factors could cause the population of woodlice to increase?

7   Human activities can cause damage to ecosystems. Look at the food web for a coral reef on page 43. Triton snails have beautiful shells and are caught by fishermen as tourist souvenirs.
    a What effect might this have on the ecosystem of the reef?
    b How could this damage be controlled?

8   Many animals can be trained to do a 'job' that helps human beings. Make a list of three different types of animal and the job that they can be trained to do.

Level 6

9 Look at the story of the Gronks, Drangs and Zooby birds on pages 40–41. Rools are similar to Drangs and feed on similar animals, but they usually live on another part of Zorb. What would be the effect on the populations of Gronks, Drangs and Zooby birds if a number of Rools were introduced to the area?

10 Boats can cause damage to the Great Barrier Reef. They can break the coral with their anchors, and propellers can cause injuries to larger animals such as turtles. They can also cause oil and petrol pollution. Suggest a design for a boat for the eco-tourism industry which has a very low impact on the reef environment.

11 If animals only had innate behaviours which were 'fixed' at birth they would be much less likely to survive. Explain why this is and why it is an advantage to be able to live and learn.

12 Defra advises farmers to 'check the TB status of farms where they buy cattle' to add to their herds.
  a What do you think Defra means by this?
  b Why is it important that farmers take this advice?

Level 7

13 The Barn Owl Trust has some rescued owls which are ready for release. They have an area in mind where they could release them. It has suitable nesting sites but there are other factors which they must consider. What are these factors and how might the Barn Owl Trust go about ensuring that the release will be successful?

14 Greg was watching an advertisement for a popular brand of beer. The people in the advertisement were all laughing and having fun and the sun was shining. Explain how this advertisement was designed to encourage Greg to buy the drink.

15 Explain how the following can help to reduce the spread of TB:
  a TB testing of cattle and of any badgers found dead.
  b special fencing around areas where cattle are kept.
  c safe storage of cattle feed that badgers might like to eat.
  d thorough cleaning of cattle feed troughs.

The International Space Station (ISS) orbits at about 380 km above the surface of the Earth. This giant structure in Space is a joint venture between several countries. Scientists from the USA, Russia, Japan, Canada and several European countries work together and share ideas to make the project a success. This is called collaboration.

Scientists with different skills and knowledge, often from different countries, will work as a team to solve the same problem. A good example of this is the investigation of the effect of weightlessness on humans in Space.

To make progress, scientists often need to develop new materials. To do this, they use their knowledge of existing materials. This knowledge is based on the properties of chemical elements and the compounds they can form. Metals and non-metals all play a part. A key challenge was to develop materials to build the ISS in Space. These materials needed to be strong, but lightweight enough to be easily transported out into Space.

Now try these

- In the ISS there are three states of matter. Examples of these are the solid structure of the station, the liquids the astronauts drink, and the gases they breathe. What are the differences between the arrangement of the particles in each state of matter?

- The ISS is built from different types of materials, which have to be transported into Space. What properties will these materials need to have?

- The same properties are important for vehicles we use on Earth. What kinds of vehicle might need these properties?

Coming up in this Chapter ...

Atoms make molecules

Metals have many uses

Without gas masks these people would have died

None of these liquids are pure substances

Learn about:

- the differences between atoms, elements and molecules
- using models to explain ideas
- what compounds are

[handwritten annotations:] H_2O — 1 molecule of water. CO_2 of carbon dioxide

▲ The Atomium in Brussels

The Atomium in Brussels is a visitor attraction. It is a model of a **molecule**. Scientists use models all the time to show us what things are like. Each of its nine spheres represents each individual **atom**. You can even go inside it.

In Year 7 you found out that solids, liquids and gases are made up of particles. Everything in the Universe is made of particles – stars, our bodies, and what we eat and drink. Some substances are made of just one type of particle, for example silver and gold. Silver and gold look very different, so their particles must be different.

Like a crime scene investigator (CSI), you are going to analyse some evidence to find out what particles are in iron and sulfur.

Two solid substances

[handwritten annotation:] elements made up only one type of atom

The photograph on the left shows what iron filings and sulfur powder look like. You can't see the individual particles, but if you could, they would look something like the diagram below.

The smallest particles of iron and sulfur are called atoms. An atom can't be broken down into anything simpler. The atoms in iron are all iron atoms. The atoms in sulfur are all sulfur atoms. When all the atoms are all the same in a substance, scientists call that substance an **element.** An atom of iron is different from an atom of sulfur, so iron and sulfur are different elements.

John Dalton, in the early nineteenth century, was the first scientist to describe the particles in substances as atoms.

▲ Iron filings and sulfur powder

[handwritten annotation:] Mixtures easily separate using a magnet

▼ The particles in iron and sulfur

Iron

Sulfur

| **A** | What do the atoms in an element have in common? (Level 4) |

[handwritten annotation:] compound can only separate by chemical means

Do you like sweets?

(handwritten: atoms → subatomic particles " " " ")

What's in a reaction?

(handwritten at top right: Neutrons / neutral, Protons / positive, Electrons / negative)

> Orange tastes all the same. It's like an element.

> Chocolate tastes all the same. It's also like an element.

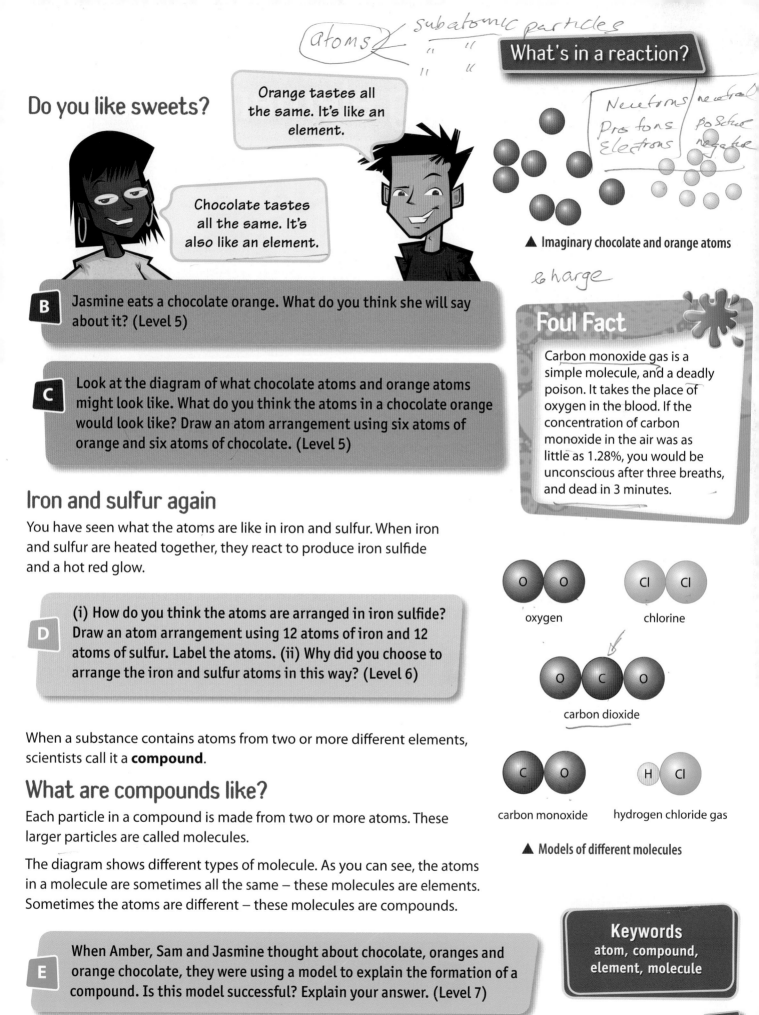

▲ Imaginary chocolate and orange atoms

(handwritten: charge)

B Jasmine eats a chocolate orange. What do you think she will say about it? (Level 5)

C Look at the diagram of what chocolate atoms and orange atoms might look like. What do you think the atoms in a chocolate orange would look like? Draw an atom arrangement using six atoms of orange and six atoms of chocolate. (Level 5)

Foul Fact

Carbon monoxide gas is a simple molecule, and a deadly poison. It takes the place of oxygen in the blood. If the concentration of carbon monoxide in the air was as little as 1.28%, you would be unconscious after three breaths, and dead in 3 minutes.

Iron and sulfur again

You have seen what the atoms are like in iron and sulfur. When iron and sulfur are heated together, they react to produce iron sulfide and a hot red glow.

D (i) How do you think the atoms are arranged in iron sulfide? Draw an atom arrangement using 12 atoms of iron and 12 atoms of sulfur. Label the atoms. (ii) Why did you choose to arrange the iron and sulfur atoms in this way? (Level 6)

oxygen

chlorine

carbon dioxide

When a substance contains atoms from two or more different elements, scientists call it a **compound**.

What are compounds like?

Each particle in a compound is made from two or more atoms. These larger particles are called molecules.

The diagram shows different types of molecule. As you can see, the atoms in a molecule are sometimes all the same – these molecules are elements. Sometimes the atoms are different – these molecules are compounds.

carbon monoxide   hydrogen chloride gas

▲ Models of different molecules

E When Amber, Sam and Jasmine thought about chocolate, oranges and orange chocolate, they were using a model to explain the formation of a compound. Is this model successful? Explain your answer. (Level 7)

Keywords
atom, compound, element, molecule

Learn about:

- what chemical symbols are used for
- how Mendeleev organised the elements
- the Periodic Table

▲ Libraries are organised so that you can easily find what you are looking for

In Japan the word for the element iron is tetsú.

In France it is fer.

In Russia it is УТЮГ

Books are carefully organised in a library. Just think how hard it would be to find a book without organisation. Scientists also organise the chemical elements.

Chemical symbols

How can scientists in different countries communicate with each other if they all use different names for the same thing? Scientists get round this problem by giving every chemical element a **symbol**.

Some elements have one letter as a symbol. The symbol for oxygen is O. Most have two letters. The symbol for iron is Fe.

A Why do scientists use symbols for chemical elements? (Level 4)

Sorting it out

In the middle of the nineteenth century, scientists had discovered about 60 elements. But they had a problem – there seemed to be no way of organising them. Most were solids, some were liquids, and some were gases.

Scientists tried to organise the elements by their properties, but they all failed. One scientist organised them in groups of three. Another used groups of seven. But when a new element was discovered, it didn't fit in, and spoiled their patterns. In 1869 a Russian chemist called Dmitri Mendeleev hit the headlines.

B Early scientists thought of different ways of organising the elements. What was the problem with their ideas? (Level 5)

Mendeleev arranged the elements in order of the mass of their atoms, and he left gaps for those that were undiscovered. His pattern allowed him to predict what these undiscovered elements would be like.

The Periodic Table — *A league of elements*

Mendeleev's creative game of cards is the basis for how the elements are organised today in the **Periodic Table**. You can see it below.

In the Periodic Table, you can see the symbols for all the known elements. Each of the vertical columns is called a **group**. They contain elements with the same kind of properties. Each horizontal row is called a **period**.

properties — behaviour appearance texture

period

elements — raw materials Everyday material/metals

What's in a reaction?

Dmitri Mendeleev liked to play cards, and this gave him the idea of using one card for each element. The cards were numbered from the element with the lightest mass to the element with the heaviest mass. He then laid out the cards so that the elements with similar properties came together in vertical columns.

Groups

▢ metals
▢ non-metals

I	II											III	IV	V	VI	VII	0
								1 H Hydrogen									2 He Helium
3 Li Lithium	4 Be Beryllium											5 B Boron	6 C Carbon	7 N Nitrogen	8 O Oxygen	9 F Fluorine	10 Ne Neon
11 Na Sodium	12 Mg Magnesium											13 Al Aluminium	14 Si Silicon	15 P Phosphorus	16 S Sulfur	17 Cl Chlorine	18 Ar Argon
19 K Potassium	20 Ca Calcium	21 Sc Scandium	22 Ti Titanium	23 V Vanadium	24 Cr Chromium	25 Mn Manganese	26 Fe Iron	27 Co Cobalt	28 Ni Nickel	29 Cu Copper	30 Zn Zinc	31 Ga Gallium	32 Ge Germanium	33 As Arsenic	34 Se Selenium	35 Br Bromine	36 Kr Krypton
37 Rb Rubidium	38 Sr Strontium	39 Y Yttrium	40 Zr Zirconium	41 Nb Niobium	42 Mo Molybdenum	43 Tc Technetium	44 Ru Ruthenium	45 Rh Rhodium	46 Pd Palladium	47 Ag Silver	48 Cd Cadmium	49 In Indium	50 Sn Tin	51 Sb Antimony	52 Te Tellurium	53 I Iodine	54 Xe Xenon
55 Cs Caesium	56 Ba Barium	57 La Lanthanum	72 Hf Hafnium	73 Ta Tantalum	74 W Tungsten	75 Re Rhenium	76 Os Osmium	77 Ir Iridium	78 Pt Platinum	79 Au Gold	80 Hg Mercury	81 Tl Thallium	82 Pb Lead	83 Bi Bismuth	84 Po Polonium	85 At Astatine	86 Rn Radon
87 Fr Francium	88 Ra Radium	89 Ac Actinium	104 Rf Rutherfordium	105 Db Dubnium	106 Sg Seaborgium	107 Bh Bohrium	108 Hs Hassium	109 Mt Meitnerium	110 Ds Darmstadtium	111 Rg Roentgenium	112 UUb	114 UUq					

Periods (1–7 shown on right)

Group

C Ryan thinks the element with the symbol C is a metal. Jasmine disagrees. Who is right? Explain your answer. (Level 5)

D Sam thinks that oxygen and nitrogen should be in the same group. What is the evidence both for and against his idea? (Level 6)

New elements

Iron — ferric ferrous

Teams of scientists are still finding new elements. These elements are very, very rare – that is why it takes so long to find them. When scientists discover a new element, they write about their discovery in a scientific publication. The element is given a temporary name with '-ium' at the end. Scientists can only give a newly discovered element a real name after its existence has been confirmed by a different team of scientists.

Element 111 was discovered in 1994. It was given a temporary name, unununium (un-un-un-ium). Its temporary symbol was the first letters of these words, Uuu. In 2006 it was given a permanent name, roentgenium.

J Newlands 1864 1869
Dimitri Mendeleev MAIN

Interesting fact

All the letters of the alphabet are used in the Periodic Table, except one – J.

E How can the Periodic Table be used to predict the properties of elements that haven't been discovered yet? (Level 7)

Keywords
group, period, Periodic Table, symbol

4.4 Metals for the future

Learn about:

- what metals are like and what they are used for
- why mercury is a hazardous metal
- what risk assessments are and why scientists do them

▲ This metallurgist is testing a metal that could give extra protection to armoured vehicles

▲ Different metals have different properties and uses

People have been using different **metals** for centuries. Gold was the first metal that was used. Pure gold occurs naturally. Some gold has been found in caves in Spain that was used about 42 000 years ago.

A scientist who works with metals is called a **metallurgist**. In the sixteenth century, Georg Agricola wrote a book called *De re metallica* (*On the nature of metals*) about the science and extraction of metals. Agricola has been called the 'father of **metallurgy**'. Today, metallurgy is an important field of science. Most universities offer degree courses in metallurgy, which can lead to a whole range of careers.

Metals are used for many different things. You find them at home, at school, in factories, in shops and on the roads. It is hard to think of a place where we don't find metals. Metals are used so much because they are good at doing so many things. A lot of the metal objects we use are made of pure metal.

> **A** What does a metallurgist do? (Level 4)

Properties of metals

Look at the diagram on the left showing metals being used for different things.

> **B** Describe the properties of metals shown in the diagrams. (Level 5)

Popular metals

Some metals are used a lot more than others. This is because they are better at doing some things than others because they have particular properties.

Some popular metals		
Metal	**What it looks like**	**Properties**
copper		excellent conductor of electricity heavier than aluminium
aluminium		excellent conductor of electricity and heat light in weight flexible strong a lot more expensive than iron
iron		strong hard dense cheap
gold		excellent conductor of electricity very expensive

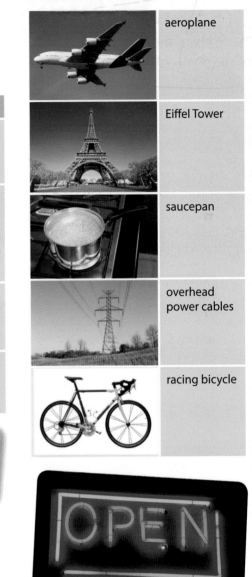

	aeroplane
	Eiffel Tower
	saucepan
	overhead power cables
	racing bicycle

C The photos on the right show objects made from different metals. (i) Choose the best metal for each object from the above table of popular metals. (ii) Give a reason for each choice. (Level 6)

A special metal

Most metals are solid at room temperature. Mercury is the exception – at room temperature it is a liquid. It melts at −39 °C. Most metals melt at very high temperatures. Tungsten melts at 3000 °C.

Some people want to ban mercury because it is very toxic. If you breathe mercury in, or eat it, it can cause breathing difficulties, hallucinations, memory loss or even death.

Scientists who use mercury have to carry out a **risk assessment**. This means they use information about the hazards to reduce the risk to human health.

The US Environmental Protection Agency has announced plans to regulate the amount of mercury released into the atmosphere from coal-fired power stations. The problem is that the mercury gets into the sea, and then into seafood. When humans eat the seafood, they absorb the poisonous mercury. Mercury levels are monitored in the air, seawater, seafood and humans.

▲ Mercury is used to give colour in these advertising lights

Foul Fact

In the nineteenth century, mercury was used to make hats out of felt. The people who made the hats often went mad, giving rise to the saying 'as mad as a hatter'.

D Some farmers keep cows in fields close to coal-burning power stations. (i) Explain why the grass, the cows and their milk should be monitored for mercury levels. (ii) Suggest control measures that the government could use. (Level 7)

Keywords
metal, metallurgist, metallurgy, risk assessment

Learn about:

- what non-metals are like, and what they are used for
- the differences between metals and non-metals
- new materials for special uses

▲ No smoke without brimstone! A volcano releasing lava and gas

Useful non-metals

Non-metal	What it looks like	Use
chlorine		chlorine is used in swimming pools
sulfur		sulfur is used to make gunpowder
carbon		carbon fibres are used in Formula 1 racing cars
phosphorus		phosphorus is used in safety matches

You find sulfur where you find volcanoes. Sulfur is a **non-metal**. Long ago, it used to be called brimstone. Not many elements are non-metals. Look back at the Periodic Table on page 55. Most non-metals are gases, one is a liquid, and the rest are solids. The properties of non-metals are usually the opposite of the properties of metals.

A How many non-metals are liquid? (Level 4)

Uses of non-metals

Although there are fewer non-metals than metals, they have a lot of important uses. The table on the left shows some of the most important non-metals and their uses.

B Suggest an important property of phosphorus that makes it suitable to use in safety matches. (Level 5)

Think back to metals

C Look at the diagram showing properties of metals on page 56. Now look at the diagram on page 59, showing properties of non-metals. Describe the properties of non-metals that each of these pictures shows. (Level 5)

Foul Fact

Chlorine gas is a deadly poison. In the First World War it was used to kill troops. It was released into the trenches and, because it is denser than air, it filled up the trenches and killed the troops inside.

▲ Non-metals have different properties from metals

Metal or non-metal?

Imagine that scientists discover eight new elements. The table shows their properties.

Jasmine, Becca and Ryan have different ideas about how to decide which of these elements are non-metals and which are metals. Jasmine suggests, 'Put all the solids in one group. Metals are solids. All the others will be non-metals.'

'No. I think we should put all those that conduct heat in one group. Metals conduct heat. All the others will be non-metals,' says Ryan.

Becca disagrees with them both. 'Put all those that conduct electricity in one group. Metals conduct electricity. All the others will be non-metals,' she says.

Elements and their properties				
Element	State at 25 °C	Shiny?	Conducts heat?	Conducts electricity?
A	solid	yes	yes	yes
B	solid	yes	yes	yes
C	liquid	no	no	no
D	solid	no	no	yes
E	solid	yes	yes	yes
F	solid	no	no	no
G	gas	no	no	no
H	solid	yes	yes	yes

D (i) For each of Jasmine, Becca and Ryan, make a list of which elements they have decided are metals and which they have decided are non-metals. (ii) Explain who has the best idea. (Level 6)

E One of the non-metal elements has an unusual property. Explain which one it is. (Level 7)

▲ The Eurofighter is a state-of-the-art fighter plane

New materials from non-metals

Scientists are able to make new materials from non-metals. Carbon fibres are made from carbon. Carbon is a weak, brittle substance, but carbon fibres are very strong and very light. The body of the Eurofighter is strengthened with a large proportion of carbon fibres. As well as making the plane strong and light, the carbon fibres make its body hard for radar to detect, so the enemy doesn't know where it is.

Keyword
non-metal

4.6 Let's get together

Learn about:

- how compounds are different from their elements
- how word equations model what is happening in a reaction

▲ International Space Station here we come!

Elements and compounds	
Elements	**Compound**
silver + chlorine	silver chloride
copper + oxygen	copper oxide
iron + sulfur	iron sulfide

The Space Shuttle transports people and materials to the ISS. The Space Shuttle uses liquid oxygen and liquid hydrogen to help it launch into Space. The waste product from the reaction is hydrogen oxide, also known as water.

Elements and compounds

You will remember that a compound is made up from a combination of more than one kind of element. The table on the left shows some elements, and compounds made from them.

Foul Fact

Volcanic activity under two lakes in the African country Cameroon produces carbon dioxide. The gas dissolves in the water. The levels of carbon dioxide can become so high that the gas is released with an explosive force. This happened in the 1980s, and more than 1000 people died.

A Name the elements in water. (Level 4)

B (i) Which elements in the table are metals and which are non-metals? (ii) What do you notice about the names of the compounds? (Level 5)

What's going on?

The table on page 61 shows some of the properties of the compound sodium chloride and the elements from which it is made.

Properties of sodium, chlorine and sodium chloride			
Substance	Sodium	Chlorine	Sodium chloride
element/compound	element	element	compound
symbol/formula	Na	Cl	NaCl
appearance	 shiny, silver solid	green gas	colourless crystals

Sodium is a metal. Because it reacts violently with water, it is stored under oil.

Chlorine is a green gas. It is a deadly poison. When sodium reacts with chlorine, it makes sodium chloride or common table salt. You can eat sodium chloride.

You can see that when elements react together, the compound produced has very different properties from the properties of its elements. Sodium and chlorine are the **reactants**. This is because they react together. Sodium chloride is the **product**. This is because it is produced in the reaction.

▲ Sodium reacts with water

C Jasmine had a dream in which she was digging in her garden and found a yellow solid. She asked a scientist to analyse it. The scientist said it was a new compound, and called it 'jasminium oxide'. What are the elements in this new compound? (Level 5)

Word equations

In some reactions, there are two reactants and one product. In other reactions, the numbers of reactants and products can be different. Sometimes there may be one reactant and two products. Sometimes there are two reactants and two products, and there are other possibilities.

Every time my teacher asks me to say what happens in a reaction, it seems to take me ages to explain.

I bet scientists have a simple way of showing what happens.

They do. They use word equations to model what happens in a reaction with the reactants and products.

D Write a word equation for what happens when sodium and chlorine react to produce sodium chloride. (Level 6)

E When sodium reacts with water, hydrogen gas is produced, and so is a compound called _____ hydroxide. (i) What is the full name of this compound? (ii) Write a word equation for the reaction. (Level 7)

Keywords
product, reactant

4.7 Mixing it up

Learn about:
- how mixtures are different from elements and compounds
- some everyday mixtures
- properties of mixtures

▲ A scuba diver breathes a mixture of gases underwater

Composition of air	
Gas	Amount in air (%)
nitrogen	78
oxygen	21
carbon dioxide	0.4
other gases	less than 1

Divers breathe the air in tanks on their back. The air contains a **mixture** of gases, including oxygen, which is essential for life. The air in the tanks is just like the air we breathe. The only difference is that the air is compressed into a liquid and put into the tanks. The liquid changes back to a gas for the scuba diver to breathe.

A What gas is most important for scuba divers to have in their tanks? (Level 4)

What's in air?

The table above shows the gases that are in air, and how much of each gas there is.

B
(i) Draw a bar graph to show the composition of air.
(ii) What gas is present in air in the largest quantity? (Level 5)

argon	hydrogen
oxygen	nitrogen
carbon	

A closer look at air

Air is a mixture of different gases. These gases do not join together to form a compound. They are just jumbled up together. Scientists say that a mixture is made up of different molecules or atoms mixed together to form a substance. The diagram on the left shows the molecules and atoms that make up air.

C Look at the diagram. Which gases are elements, and which are compounds? (Level 5)

▲ The molecules and atoms in air

Other mixtures

Some of the mixtures that people use every day include petrol, milk and beer. Even the water we drink is not **pure** water. That means it is not made up of just water molecules. It has other substances dissolved in it. Take a look at the label on the bottle of mineral water.

D The label shows that there are six metals in the water. (i) Name the six metals. (ii) Draw a bar chart for those metals with a concentration greater than 1.0 mg/l. (iii) If you drank the whole bottle of water, how much Ca would you drink? (Level 6)

NATURAL MINERAL WATER

1.5 LITRE ℮

TYPICAL ANALYSIS mg/l:

Ca	35.0	HCO_3	136.0	F	<0.1
Mg	8.5	Cl	7.5	Fe	<0.01
Na	6.0	SO_4	6.0	Al	<0.01
K	0.6	NO_3	<0.1	T.D.S at 100°C	136

CHLORINE FREE   pH at source 7.8
LOW MINERAL CONTENT.
SUITABLE FOR A LOW SODIUM DIET.
ONCE OPENED STORE IN REFRIGERATOR
AND USE WITHIN 7 DAYS.

▲ The composition of natural mineral water

Mixtures with the same name may be made up of different amounts of each substance. Seawater is a mixture, but the seawater in different seas is not the same. The Dead Sea contains nine times as much salt as the Mediterranean Sea.

E Two different companies both make a fizzy drink that they call 'cola'. Explain why cola is a mixture, and how the two colas might be different from each other. (Level 7)

Foul Fact

Some of the water molecules you have drunk today could once have been drunk by Julius Caesar. Even worse – think about what happened to them in his body, and how they got to you!

Pure substance or mixture?

A pure substance has one **melting point** and one **boiling point**. If other substances are added to a pure substance, then its melting point and boiling point change. When water is boiled and different amounts of salt are added to the water, the boiling point increases. The results in the table show this.

Changing boiling points

Substance	Boiling point (°C)
water (100 cm³)	100
water (100 cm³) + salt (5 g)	101
water (100 cm³) + salt (25 g)	105
water (100 cm³) + salt (50 g)	110

▶ Distilling salty water

Pure water

The photo shows **distillation** of salty water. Salty water is a mixture. You can get pure water from it when you distil it.

Keywords
boiling point, distillation, melting point, mixture, pure

4.8 Producing chemicals

Learn about:
- the chemicals industry
- developing new chemicals
- predicting how chemicals will react

▲ A lot of different chemicals are manufactured in this plant

▲ Chemicals are needed to make all these products

The chemicals industry converts raw materials into more than 70 000 different chemicals, which are used by manufacturers all over the world. One very important raw material is crude oil.

The chemicals industry is a very important industry, especially in the UK and the USA. The UK chemicals industry employs about 214 000 people.

A Explain why the chemicals industry is so important. (Level 4)

New chemicals

John is a chemical engineer. He works in the Research and Development Department of a large chemical plant.

Foul Fact

Raw materials can be dangerous. When a tanker called *Exxon Valdez* hit a reef off the coast of Alaska in 1989, tonnes of crude oil were spilled into the sea. Thousands of birds and animals died.

We are developing new chemicals all the time. I use lots of different chemical processes to produce new materials. We then test them to make sure they are safe and work as they are supposed to.

B What do scientists need to carry out before they start working with a new chemical? (Level 5)

It is important for chemical engineers to be able to predict how different chemicals will react. To do this, scientists need to know the **chemical properties** of the different chemicals.

In an oil refinery, crude oil is split up into a lot of different chemicals, which can be used for different purposes. One example is the gas ethene. Ethene is a small molecule. When a lot of ethene molecules are joined together in a long chain, they make polythene, which is a plastic. The properties of polythene are different from the properties of ethene.

Many chemicals react in a similar way in chemical reactions. This means that scientists can usually work out what new materials will be made in a reaction, even before they carry it out. When elements react with oxygen, they make oxides. In a similar way, elements that react with sulfur make sulfides. Hydrogen reacts with sulfur to make hydrogen sulfide.

C Predict what will be made when (i) copper reacts with oxygen, and (ii) magnesium reacts with sulfur. (iii) Write word equations for the two reactions. (Level 5)

Names of compounds	
Compound contains	**Compound name**
chlorine	chloride
bromine	bromide

The table on the right shows some more examples.

D (i) Fluorine is similar to chlorine and bromine. Predict what its compound name will be. (ii) Predict the products of sodium with chlorine, bromine and fluorine, and write the word equation for each reaction. (Level 6)

When things go wrong

Do you live near a chemical plant? A lot of people do. Chemical plants can be good for jobs and the local economy. But the chemicals they use, and produce, can pollute the local environment. And if something goes wrong at the plant, the consequences can be serious.

In 1974, an explosion at a chemical plant near the village of Flixborough in Lincolnshire killed 28 people and injured 36 more. The blast damaged about 1800 houses and other buildings near the plant.

▲ In 1984 a poisonous gas leaked from the Union Carbide chemical plant in Bhopal, India, and thousands of people died

E If there was an oil refinery on your doorstep, there would be potential hazards. Explain what some of these hazards might be, and suggest ways in which the oil refinery could minimise the risks. (Level 7)

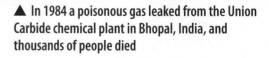

Keyword
chemical property

4.9 For good or evil

Learn about:
- the advantages and disadvantages of science
- ethical and moral decisions

▶ Science can be used to harm people

Not all scientific developments have a peaceful purpose. Many are unethical and immoral. Chemical warfare was started by the invading Germans in about 1915 in France. During the First World War, both sides developed and used different harmful gases as **chemical weapons**. Mustard gas produces large, mustard-coloured blisters both outside and inside the body, making it is hard to breathe and speak. The photo shows a victim of mustard gas.

Other gases such as tear gas, chlorine and phosgene were also used. Phosgene is very toxic and caused most deaths. The First World War became known as 'the chemists' war'.

 A Which chemical weapon caused the most deaths in the First World War? (Level 4)

Chemical and nuclear weapons

In the Second World War, nerve gases were used. These were even more deadly than the gases used in the First World War. Scientists also developed the atomic bomb during the Second World War. Atomic bombs were dropped on Hiroshima and Nagasaki in Japan in 1945, killing many thousands of people.

The most recent known use of chemical weapons was during the Iran–Iraq war in the 1970s. Iraqi forces attacked a city in Iraq called Halabja with mustard gas and nerve gas. The city contained Iranian forces and Iraqi rebels, but it also contained a lot of civilians. Thousands of people died. Today there are international agreements between most nations not to use chemical weapons.

▲ Science gave us the atomic bomb

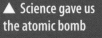

B What type of bomb caused thousands of deaths in the Second World War? (Level 4)

C Which parts of the body do you think nerve gases attack? (Level 5)

All countries should destroy all their chemical weapons as soon as they can.

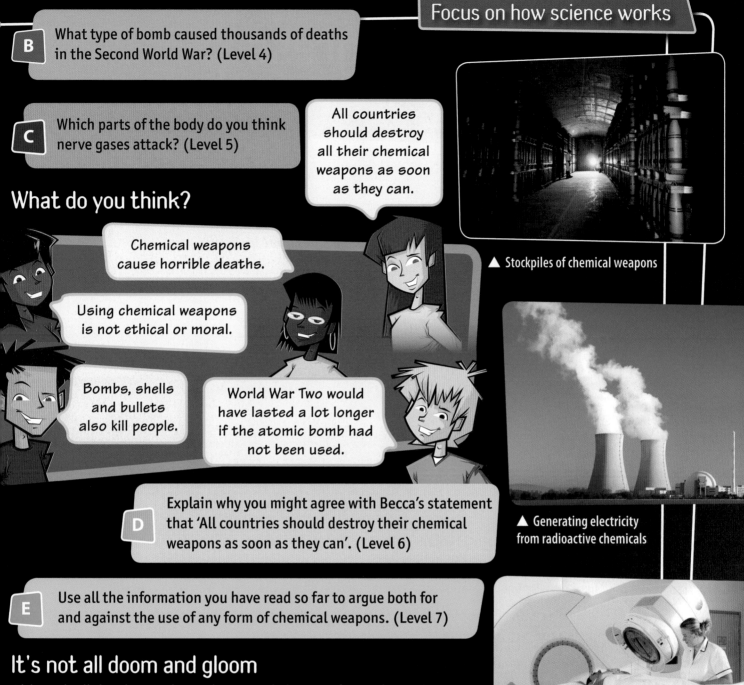

▲ Stockpiles of chemical weapons

What do you think?

Chemical weapons cause horrible deaths.

Using chemical weapons is not ethical or moral.

Bombs, shells and bullets also kill people.

World War Two would have lasted a lot longer if the atomic bomb had not been used.

▲ Generating electricity from radioactive chemicals

D Explain why you might agree with Becca's statement that 'All countries should destroy their chemical weapons as soon as they can'. (Level 6)

E Use all the information you have read so far to argue both for and against the use of any form of chemical weapons. (Level 7)

It's not all doom and gloom

Although all the chemicals you have read about so far are hazardous, many of them have very important uses. The photo shows a **nuclear power** plant. It uses radioactive chemicals to produce electricity. In the UK, we generate about 20% of our electricity using nuclear power.

Doctors treat people who have cancer with **radiotherapy**. The chemicals in the radioactive source give out radiation that treats tumours. Risk assessments are carried out in hospitals for the benefit of both staff and patients. In this case, the risk of exposure to different levels of radiation, or different times of exposure, would be assessed.

Even phosgene and chlorine are useful. Their major use is in the manufacture of plastics. Phosgene is used to make polycarbonate, which is used for conservatory roofs.

▲ Radioactive chemicals can help to treat cancer

Keywords
chemical weapon, nuclear power, radiotherapy

Assess your progress

Level 4

1 a What did Mendeleev call his organisation of the elements?
  b What are the symbols for oxygen and iron?

2 Name a very strong, but cheap, metal.

3 On which side of the Periodic Table do you find non-metals?

4 Explain what a mixture is.

Level 5

5 Helium is an element. Helium atoms are not joined together. Draw a diagram of the arrangement of atoms in helium gas.

6 Explain why Dmitri Mendeleev's organisation of the elements was so successful.

7 Why are carbon fibres, rather than a metal, used to make the body of a Formula 1 racing car?

8 Predict the names of the products for reactions between the following elements:
a hydrogen and oxygen; b copper and oxygen; c potassium and chlorine.

9 The diagram shows six different gases.

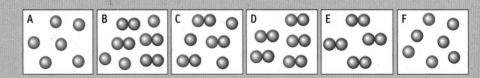

Which of the gases are: a atoms; b molecules;
c elements; d compounds; e mixtures?

10 Explain why the First World War was called the 'chemists' war'.

Level 6

11 Look at the Periodic Table on page 55. **a** Why do you think there is no element 113 or 115? **b** Use the key to give element 115 a temporary name.

zero = nil	one = un	two = bi
three = tri	four = quad	five = pent
six = hex	seven = sept	eight = oct

12 Suggest why the bodies of the Stealth Bomber and Eurofighter are made of similar materials.

13 Three liquids, X, Y and Z, all have the same name but different boiling points. X boils at 80 °C, Y at 82 °C and Z at 84 °C. Which liquid, X, Y or Z, is the purest? Explain your answer.

14 Explain why ethene and polyethene have different chemical properties.

15 What problems could result from placing an industrial site producing plastics from phosgene in an area where lots of people live?

Level 7

16 Imagine that in 2020 a space mission to Mars discovers a large supply of a new metal. The metal is stronger and lighter than any metal known previously. It has all the other properties of metals. What purposes could this metal be used for? Give reasons for your choices.

17 Look at the information in the table about the elements silicon, phosphorus and boron.

Element	State at 25 °C	Colour	Shiny?	Conducts electricity?	Conducts thermal energy?
silicon	solid	grey	yes	no	yes
phosphorus	solid	black	no	yes	no
boron	solid	grey	no	no	yes

For each of these elements, say whether you think it is a metal or a non-metal. Explain your answers.

18 Orange juice is a mixture. Which statement, A, B, C or D, is the best description of this mixture? Explain your answer.
A It is safe to drink.
B It always contains the same proportions of each ingredient.
C It has different ingredients, which can be in different amounts.
D It is a single, pure substance.

5.1 A leap in time

If you were a polar explorer in 1908 then you would have had to wear bulky clothes to keep you warm. These clothes were heavy which made moving around difficult.

Since then, there have been 100 years of scientific progress. Scientists have developed new technologies which have led to improvements in polar explorers' clothing and equipment.

The same technological developments that have given modern polar explorers hi-tech clothing have also given us winter clothing which is warm, but light.

Now try these

- Make a list of animals that live at the North or South Pole. How do they survive the cold?

- Make a list of the different ways you keep warm during cold weather, both in your home and when you go out.

- Imagine that you have put some ice cubes in a pan and heated them. Describe as many changes as you can that happen to the cubes before the pan is empty.

ifferent coloured oils rise and fall
n lava lamps

Why does this chef need a cloth to hold this pan?

The Space Shuttle was a great scientific leap forward

This amazing material keeps this person from burning their hand

Learn about:

● what scientists mean by heat and temperature
● how to test a theory

▲ What is the quickest way to boil carrots?

▲ Ryan and Becca are testing a theory by doing an experiment

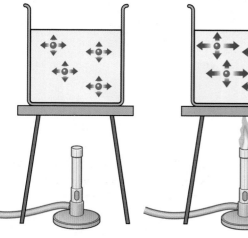
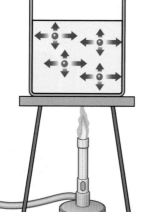

▲ Water particles move around more when they are heated

Becca and Ryan are cooking for their friends. They are going to boil some carrots to have with chicken. 'The carrots will boil quicker if we cover them with lots of water in the pan,' says Ryan. Becca disagrees. 'No, I think the carrots will boil quicker if we cover them with only a small amount of water.'

They decide to do an experiment to find out whose **theory** is correct. They start cooking the same amount of carrots at the same time in two identical pans. Both pans are heated by identical flames. Ryan's pan has a lot of water in it while Becca's has only a little water. The water in Becca's pan begins to boil and cook the carrots first.

You need to know the difference between **heat** and **temperature** to understand why. Using the particle model of matter will help.

Modelling energy

In Year 7 we said that all matter is made up of particles. These particles are vibrating all the time. This vibration is what we call heat or **thermal energy**. When we heat something the energy is transferred to the particles, which makes them vibrate or move around more. The diagram shows what happens when you heat water in a beaker.

> **A** What is the difference between particles in carrots at 50 °C and particles in carrots at 80 °C? (Level 4)

The graph shows what happens to the temperature of the water in Ryan's and Becca's pans when they are heated. Notice how one pan heats up far more quickly than the other. This is because there is less water in it so the energy is transferred to fewer particles.

B (i) Why does the temperature on the graph start at 20 °C? (ii) How long does it take for Becca's pan with the smaller volume of water to boil? (Level 4)

C How much longer does Ryan's pan take to boil? (Level 5)

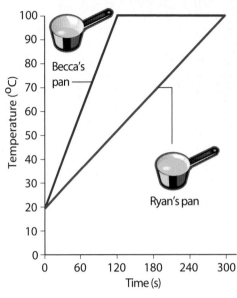

▲ How quickly the temperature rose

Heat and temperature

Using the particle model, we can explain the difference between heat and temperature.

If you heat two beakers of water for the same time using identical Bunsen burners, each beaker receives the same amount of energy. This energy is measured in **joules**. Heat is a measure of the total amount of energy in the water.

If one beaker has less water in it, the temperature will be higher because the energy is shared out among fewer particles. Temperature is a measure of the energy per particle and is measured in **°C**.

D Explain, in terms of particles, why the iceberg has more heat energy than the molten iron. (Level 6)

E A red-hot iron nail (temperature 1010 °C) is dropped into a large bath of cold water, at 10 °C. By how much do you think the temperature of the water will increase? Choose from A, B or C and then justify your answer. A – a tiny amount B – 500 °C C – 1000 °C (Level 7)

▲ There is more heat energy in a large iceberg than in a small piece of molten iron even though the iron is hotter

Keywords
°C, heat, joules, temperature, theory, thermal energy

73

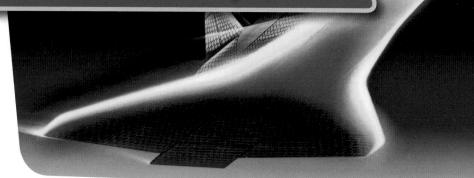

Learn about:

- how heat travels through solids
- how the space shuttle protects its astronauts

▲ The Space Shuttle entering the Earth's atmosphere

You might think it is easy to enter the Earth's atmosphere – just fall in from Space. Wrong! The atmosphere causes problems that scientists have had to overcome. If you look at the photo of the space shuttle you can see that one of the major problems is heat.

A Look at the photo of the shuttle. Where do you think is the hottest part? Explain your answer. (Level 4)

The problems

Sonya Young is training to be an astronaut. In a few months' time she will be sent up in the shuttle to the International Space Station. 'When an object enters the atmosphere it gets hot. This is because it rubs against the particles in the air. When things rub together, they always produce heat. This is because of friction' she explains.

You might not get hot walking through the air but the Shuttle enters the atmosphere at 26 700 km/h. Without a heat shield it would get so hot inside the shuttle that the astronauts would be killed.

B Why does the speed of the shuttle make it hot as it flies through the air? (Level 5)

Try rubbing your hands together for a while to see how rubbing things produces heat.

Conduction

Thermal energy (heat) moves through solids by a process called **conduction**. The body of the Shuttle is made of metal. Metals are good **conductors** of heat. This is because when they are heated, the particles in the metal start to vibrate more. The particles are close together and as they collide energy is transferred through the metal.

When scientists were developing the Shuttle they needed to find a way of stopping the heat passing into the cockpit of the shuttle from its metal body.

C If you touch a piece of metal on a cold day it feels much colder than a piece of wood. Explain why. (Hint: remember that your hand is warm.) (Level 6)

▲ Heat energy is transferred along the rod by the particles vibrating and colliding

The material for the job

The NASA scientists developed special tiles made from silicon, which is made from sand. These were stuck onto the outside of the Shuttle. When one side of these special tiles is being heated, you can hold the other side and not get burnt. So how do these tiles work?

The tiles work by trapping a lot of air which reduces the heat travelling through them. Air is an **insulator**. Conduction does not happen in gases such as air. This is because the particles are far apart. When they vibrate it is much harder for them to collide with another particle than it is for the particles in a solid. Non-metals are also poor conductors but they still let some heat pass through.

◀ Hundreds of silicon tiles protect the Space Shuttle astronauts when they enter the Earth's atmosphere

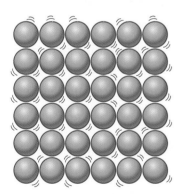

▲ Metal particles are held together in rows, touching each other and vibrating on the spot

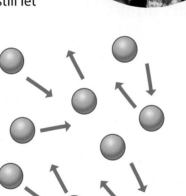

▲ Gas particles are not held together but are far apart, disordered and zoom about

D Glass is not a good insulator. Suggest what the Shuttle designers could do to reduce heat entering through the windows at the front of the Shuttle during entry into the Earth's atmosphere? (Level 7)

▲ The Space Shuttle tiles do not conduct heat energy

E When the Shuttle is orbiting in space the temperature outside the Shuttle is about −270°C. What is the job of the insulating tiles now? (Level 7)

Keywords
conduction, conductor, insulator

Learn about:

- how the particle model explains how heat travels in liquids and gases
- why it is cooler on the coast in summer

Scientists at work

Scientists who are involved in forecasting the weather are called meteorologists. They often use complex computer models of convection.

We hope that a fire like the one in the photo will never happen in your house. In a fire smoke travels across the top of the room. This is because it is being carried by hot air. If you were in this room the fire brigade would advise you to crawl across the floor because it is cooler and there is less smoke there. But why do smoke and heat rise?

They rise because of how heat travels in liquids and gases. This is a process that scientists call **convection**.

Particles again

Hot air rises because of particles. The particle model shows that, unlike particles in a solid, particles in a gas are free to move around.

Energy is transferred by heat to the gas particles and they move away from each other. This makes the gas less **dense** as the particles are now further apart. The particles move upwards through the particles above them. These colder particles are closer together, making this part of the gas denser than the heated gas, so they move downwards. Scientists call this motion a **convection current**. During a fire the bits of soot in the smoke are carried up with the hottest air.

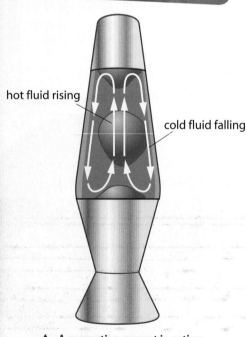

hot fluid rising

cold fluid falling

▲ A convection current in action

A In what direction do hot and cold gases move? (Level 4)

B What happens to particles when an object is heated? (Level 5)

By the seaside

It's Saturday and it's hot, hot, hot! We've decided to go to the seaside.

But why is it that after you battle your way through the traffic jams to the coast, then open the car door ready to run to the beach, it's freezing?

Why do you nearly always get a cool wind at the coast? On a sunny day the land heats up faster than the sea. The air above the land gets warmer and rises. The air above the sea is colder. It falls and blows across the coast to replace the hot air.

C How could this breeze be used to help produce electricity? (Level 5)

▲ When the air in a hot air balloon is heated the balloon rises

Cooling convection

San Francisco is on the west coast of America, close to a desert which produces a lot of hot air. The air above the Pacific Ocean next to San Francisco is much cooler and it is often foggy there. San Jose is another town just 15 miles inland. The table shows the average temperatures of the two cities in different months.

City temperatures						
City	Average temperature (°C)					
	January	March	May	July	September	November
San Francisco	14	16	16	17	18	17
San Jose	15	23	27	29	26	18

D (i) Plot a graph of the average temperatures for each city and describe how the temperatures vary over a year.
(ii) Explain, using the idea of convection, why San Francisco's average temperature is different from San Jose's average temperature. (Level 6)

▲ The ice cube stays cool even when some of the water in the test tube is boiling

The amazing non-melting ice cube

Convection happens in liquids in the same way that it happens in gases. Look at the diagram of the ice cube in a test tube. The water at the top of the tube is boiling but the ice does not melt.

▶ Kettles usually have their heating element at the bottom

E Use the idea of particles to explain why the ice cube does not melt. (Level 6)

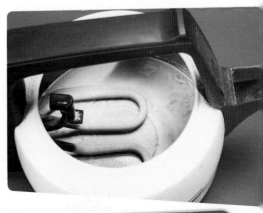

F Look at the photo of the kettle. Explain in as much detail as you can what would happen if the heating element were put near the top of a kettle. (Level 7)

Keywords
convection, convection current, dense

Learn about:

- the three states of matter
- why things melt
- what plasma is
- how different scientists build on information from others

▲ What has caused the snowman to melt?

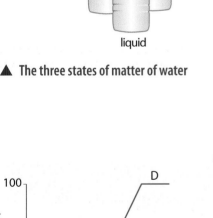

solid

liquid

gas

▲ The three states of matter of water

All good things must come to an end. When the day warms up, the snowman **melts**. To understand why the frozen water changes back to a **liquid**, we need to know how particles behave in the different **states of matter**.

The states of matter

Water is a liquid at room temperature, but put it in the freezer and it turns into a **solid**. Heat it for long enough and it turns into a **gas**. Scientists say that solid, liquid and gas are the three states of matter.

A Look at the diagram showing the three states of matter of water. Copy the diagram. Write a label next to each arrow choosing the words from this list: boil, melt, freeze, condense. (Level 4)

From ice to steam

I have been heating some ice in a beaker. First I crushed the ice. Then I took the temperature every 2 minutes. My results are shown in the graph.

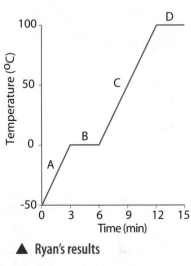

▲ Ryan's results

B (i) Take a look at the graph showing Ryan's results. What is happening to the water during section B?
(ii) How long does it take the ice to melt? (Level 5)

C By how much is the water's temperature increasing per minute during section C? (Level 6)

◀ One model of the solid state of matter

Why do things change state?

The particles in a solid are joined together by forces. One way to model this would be for you and your friends to walk around linking arms.

When you heat a solid, its particles gain energy and the energy increases. When the solid reaches its melting point, energy is used to break the forces between the particles instead of increasing the temperature. The solid becomes a liquid. Once all the forces are broken the temperature of the liquid increases.

If you continue to heat the liquid, the particles gain enough energy to leave the surface of the liquid and you have a gas.

▲ Plasma TV sets were first developed by Donald Bitzer and Gene Slottow in 1964

Plasma

Plasma is an electrically charged gas which is usually at a very high temperature. Scientists call it the fourth state of matter because it has different properties from an ordinary gas. Sir William Crookes saw it first in 1879 and called it 'radiant matter'. Sir J J Thomson discovered what it was in 1897 and it was named 'plasma' in 1928 by Irving Langmuir. Scientific knowledge is usually built up piece by piece like this.

Lightning and the Aurora Borealis (the Northern Lights) are examples of natural plasma. Artificially produced plasma is used in plasma TV sets.

Interesting fact

99% of all the matter in the Universe is plasma, including all the stars.

D In Ryan's experiment, explain why the temperature stops increasing when the ice is melting. (Level 7)

E You can model a solid by linking arms with your class mates. Describe how your class could model liquids and gases. (Level 7)

Keywords
gas, liquid, melt, plasma, solid, state of matter

Learn about:

- how heat energy travels through space
- how scientists can use the properties of infrared radiation
- why clothes dry on a washing line

▲ This solar power station harnesses the Sun's energy

In March 2007 the first commercial solar power station opened in Seville, Spain. It has 624 movable mirrors which focus the Sun's energy onto the top of a tower. At the top the energy turns water to steam. This turns a turbine which makes electricity.

Energy through space

How does the Sun's energy get to the mirrors? There are no particles in space so the heat cannot travel from the Sun to the Earth by conduction or convection. There has to be a method of transferring heat energy that does not need particles.

There is a method: scientists call it **radiation**. All hot objects, including people, give off **infrared radiation**. This is what we call heat. The police use special infrared cameras which detect heat to track people at night.

▲ People show up brightly on infrared cameras because they are sources of heat

> **A** Explain why thermal energy transfer by conduction or convection cannot happen in space. (Level 4)

> **B** Why do the police use infrared cameras to track people at night? (Level 5)

Reflecting radiation

If you have ever visited a hot country, you may have noticed that most houses are painted a light colour. This is because radiation **reflects** off shiny or light coloured surfaces. The people inside the houses are kept cool.

Shiny surfaces can also be used to keep people warm. You often see marathon runners wrapped in foil after a race. This foil reflects back their body heat so they don't cool down too quickly.

C Two pieces of paper are placed on some snow. One piece is black and the other is white. Under which piece of paper will the snow melt more quickly? Explain your answer. (Level 6)

D Some scientists think that if the ice at the North Pole melts and is replaced by dark blue ocean then this will add to global warming. Explain why they think this. (Hint: think about colour.) (Level 7)

▲ Keeping warm after a race

Letting the heat through

Jasmine has made a bad decision. She has decided to wear a black outfit on a hot, sunny day. Amber has decided to wear white because she thinks it will keep her cooler. Amber explains why.

Black, dull surfaces absorb radiation and let it pass through, so wearing dark clothes on a sunny day will make you feel very hot!

Washing day

When your clothes have been washed they need to be dried. You could put them in the clothes drier. This is quick and convenient but it costs money and uses up energy resources. Another way is to hang out the clothes on a washing line. Why do clothes dry when they never get hot enough for the water to boil? They dry because of **evaporation**.

When air blows through the clothes on a washing line, some energy transfers from the air to the wet clothes. If a particle of water in the wet clothes gets enough energy, it turns into gas and evaporates away. When you sweat your body is cooling itself by evaporation, just like the washing.

▲ Hung out to dry

E During what sort of day will clothes dry most quickly on a washing line? Explain your answer. (Level 7)

Keywords
evaporation, infrared radiation, radiation, reflect

5.7 Amazing Aerogel

Learn about:

- how new materials can help to solve problems

▲ These crayons resting on a thin sheet of Aerogel do not melt

Aerogel is a very special type of foam which is 99.8% air. It was first invented in the 1930s but was very brittle and could not be shaped. Now a team of scientists have discovered how to make it flexible so that it does not break so easily. This means there are a lot of ways in which it can be used to solve problems.

Escaping heat

Military aeroplane and helicopter engines produce a lot of heat. This means they can be attacked by heat-seeking missiles. If the engine is surrounded by a layer of Aerogel, then less heat escapes for the missiles to detect.

▲ Aerogel can be used to reduce the amount of heat from a helicopter engine

A Why do heat-seeking missiles find it hard to hit planes which have Aerogel surrounding their engines? (Level 4)

Aerogel can also be used to stop heat from escaping from hot water pipes. When heat escapes energy is wasted, which means more of the Earth's energy supplies are used up. Lots of other materials can be used to stop heat escaping, so why is Aerogel so good?

B Look at the diagram showing the insulation round a pipe. How many times better is Aerogel at insulating than fibreglass? (Level 4)

C Explain why Aerogel is such a good insulator. (Level 5)

20 cm thick fibreglass

1 cm thick Aerogel

30 cm pipe

▲ Different thicknesses of insulation required to keep the heat in a pipe

Using Aerogel to catch comet dust

Scientists look at the dust from comets to find out what the Solar System was like when it was first formed. They want to know what the dust is made of and what shape it is. But it is hard to catch the fast moving dust. If the dust rubs against anything, friction makes the dust hot which can change it. If the dust hits anything hard, that can also change its shape.

So, scientists use Aerogel in a dust collector on the *Stardust* spacecraft. As the very small dust particles go through the Aerogel they leave little paths. These paths are used to find the dust particles when the probe comes back to Earth.

dust catcher

▲ How Aerogel is used to catch comet dust

D Write down two reasons why the dust particles do not get damaged when they go into Aerogel. (Level 6)

E Think of an application of Aerogel not mentioned so far. Explain why it would be a better material for that application than the material used at the moment. (Level 7)

▶ Particle captured in Aerogel

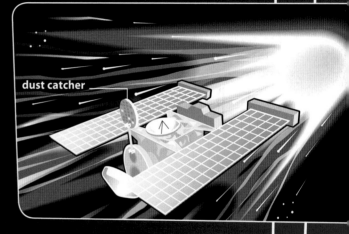

Working together

Work on new materials is often done in universities. The French government paid a university to find out if Aerogel could be used to hold rocket fuel. The work was done by a student who discovered new ways of making the gel. His work was published in scientific magazines. Other scientists read the articles and this gave them new ideas about how to use Aerogel.

Interesting fact

If your house was made of Aerogel, it would have a mass of 2 grams. This is about the same as half a teaspoonful of sugar.

Assess your progress

Level 4

1 A block of iron is heated and the temperature increases by 20 °C. If a piece of iron with double the mass is given the same amount of energy, by how much do you think the temperature will increase?

2 Why do solar power stations use a lot of mirrors?

3 Look at the graph showing Becca's and Ryan's pans being heated. Why does the temperature stop increasing at 100 °C?

4 Radiators heat a room by convection. Describe how a radiator heats an entire room.

5 What do scientists say happens when a solid turns into a liquid?

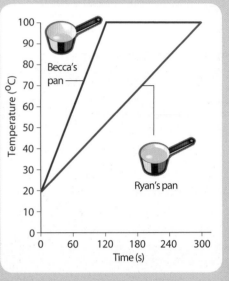

Level 5

6 If you place a lid on a pan of water while you heat it, how will this affect how quickly it boils? Explain your answer.

7 People often put duvets on their beds to keep them warm at night. A duvet acts as an insulator. Explain how it keeps people warm.

8 What would happen if you tried to heat a room with a radiator that was positioned at the top of a wall?

9 If you wanted to keep your house warm on a cold day, what colour should your walls be? Explain your answer.

10 Jasmine says that you could use a sheet of Aerogel between sheets of glass in oven doors to make them safer. Do you think she is right? Explain your answer.

11 Look at Ryan's experiment on page 78 with melting ice cubes. What could Ryan do to improve the experiment?

Level 6

12 Two beakers have water in – one beaker has twice the amount of water as the other beaker. If you heat both beakers the same amount, the temperature of the beaker with half the volume of water does not increase twice as quickly as the other beaker. Suggest why.

13 Becca is lying on the floor of the living room at home. The living room is on the ground floor. When the door is opened she feels a cold draught. Explain why this happens in as much detail as you can.

14 Sketch a graph of steam being turned into solid ice. On each section of the graph, label what is happening.

15 Aerogel is a much better insulator than fibreglass. Suggest a reason why we still use fibreglass as insulation in houses instead of using Aerogel.

16 You often see chefs on TV use a cloth to hold pans. What is the difference between their pans and the ones you use at home?

17 When it rains, the ground gets wet. Explain how it becomes dry again afterwards.

Level 7

18 a Look at Ryan's and Becca's carrot experiment on page 72. How do they make the experiment a fair test?
   b List the dependent and independent variables in the experiment.

19 Do you think conduction happens in liquids? Explain your answer using the particle model.

20 A pan of soup is placed on a cooker. Explain, in as much detail as you can, how the heat from the cooker heats up all of the soup.

21 Use the idea of particle theory to explain why a gas can spread out to fill its container?

22 Astronauts' suits are made of a light, reflective material. What might happen if they were made of a black material?

23 Thinking carefully about conditions in space, can you think of another use of Aerogel in spacecraft apart from collecting space dust? Explain your answer.

Have you ever looked up at the Moon and remembered that people walked on it as recently as 1972? They travelled there as part of the Apollo space missions. What did they leave behind?

Some of the things that were left behind are footprints, equipment and a tray of mirrors. The tray is small – just 60 cm width with 100 mirrors. It is still there and it is the only Apollo science experiment that is still running. So what is it for?

Scientists can use the mirrors to measure the distance of the Moon from the Earth and discover how this changes. They shine a very narrow beam of light at the tray and time how long it takes for the beam to return. The beam travels in a straight line to the mirror, is reflected and returns to the Earth. And here's a surprise. Scientists have discovered that the Moon is moving away from us by about 4 cm a year.

Now try these

- The Moon doesn't produce light but we can see it. Where does the Moon's light come from?

- Why did scientists put a mirror on the Moon?

- Name a kind of light that human eyes can't detect.

Coming up in this Chapter ...

...ats eyes are mirrors that
...eflect our headlights

Where do these colours
come from?

This camera sees light you
can't detect with your eyes

Telescopes help us see
stars and galaxies billions
of miles away

Learn about:

- the way that light travels
- models that help to explain how light works

▲ An awesome sight – but how do we see it?

It has taken scientists thousands of years to work out how we see. In medieval times people thought that our eyes sent out rays that hit objects and returned with information about what was out there. Now we know that light always comes from a **luminous** source such as the Sun, stars or a light bulb and not our eyes.

Travelling at light speed

The light that leaves a light bulb travels outwards in all directions. All light travels at an incredible 300 000 km per second. This is so fast that when you turn on the light, you see everything in the room at once. You can't tell that light arrives at objects near the bulb before reaching those further away.

 A When you switch on a light, why can't you tell that light falls on objects near the bulb before it falls on objects further away? (Level 4)

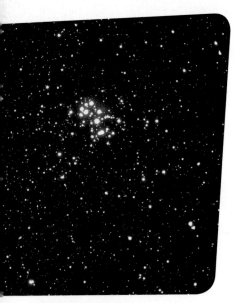

▲ The night sky contains stars that give off light, and planets that reflect it

Time taken for light to travel to you

Object	Time
your book	1/1000 000 000th of a second
Moon	1 second (approx)
Sun	8 minutes
Jupiter	35 – 52 minutes depending on whether Jupiter is on the other side of the Sun from us
the nearest star beyond our Solar System to the Earth	4 years
the brightest star in the sky, Sirius	9 years
Betelgeuse	430 years
the stars on the other side of our Galaxy	70 000 years
stars in the next nearest galaxy, Andromeda	2.5 million years

A model for light

Scientists sometimes use models to describe light. In one model, they think of light as rays and use **ray diagrams** to show the path that the light takes. Only the important rays are shown. Here's a ray diagram to explain how you see Fido.

▶ Some of the light rays from the bulb reflect off Fido's fur and travel to your eyes

B If people stand around Fido, they can all see him. Use the ray model to explain why. (Level 5)

Travelling through glass

Most materials are **opaque** – light cannot travel through them. This 'soaking up' happens with materials like wood or bricks. It is called **absorption**. Glass allows rays of light to pass through. This is called **transmission**. If the glass is clear, the rays remain organised and we can see what is on the other side of the glass. Clear glass is **transparent**.

C Draw a ray diagram to show how a girl in a room with a window as the only light source sees a clock on the wall. (Level 6)

D Use the ray model to explain what happens when light from a torch falls on a mirror made from a sheet of transparent glass with a silvery reflective layer behind it. (Level 6)

In the case of cloudy glass like a bathroom window, the rays are disorganised as they pass through. Cloudy glass is **translucent**. Light comes through the window but you can't see clearly what's on the other side.

▲ You can see clearly through transparent glass

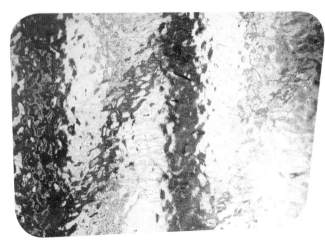

◀ You might have translucent glass in your bathroom window

Keywords
absorption, luminous, opaque, ray diagram, translucent, transmission, transparent

Learn about:

- the way that mirrors reflect light
- examples of ways we use reflected light

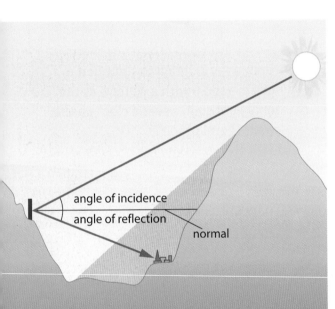

▲ This huge mirror on a mountain is eight metres by five metres

▲ A ray diagram to show what happens when a light ray arrives at a mirror and is reflected

What do you do if your village is nestled in a valley, between steep mountains, and shaded from sunlight for three months every year?

That was the problem faced by the villagers in Viganella, Italy. The tall mountains around it place it in shadow all winter. 'It was like Siberia', the villagers explained.

Then the Mayor had an idea – to install a very large mirror on the mountainside opposite to reflect the Sun's rays into the village square. It may sound crazy – but it works.

Getting the mirror's angle right

The Viganella mirror has a computer-operated motor to make sure it is always at the right angle. But what is the right angle? When scientists designed the mirror, they drew diagrams of light rays arriving at a mirror. They then drew in a line that was perpendicular to the mirror, called the **normal**.

A Why does the mirror change its angle during the day? (Level 4)

The **angle of incidence** is the angle at which light arrives at the mirror. It is measured to the normal. The **angle of reflection** is the angle at which light leaves the mirror, also measured to the normal. When light is reflected from a mirror, the angle of incidence always equals the angle of reflection. The computer uses this equation to help it work out the correct angle for the mirror.

B If the angle between a ray coming to the mirror and the reflected ray going from the mirror is 60 degrees, what is the angle of incidence? (Level 5)

C Look at the diagram showing the mirror and the village. If the patch of reflected light shines below the village on the mountainside, should the mirror be tilted more towards the Sun or away? (Level 5)

If you look in a mirror you can see your reflection, but if you look at a sheet of white paper, you can't. Both reflect light, so what is the difference between them?

How mirrors work

The answer to Ryan's question is that the mirror's surface is smooth and reflects light evenly. The paper scatters the light.

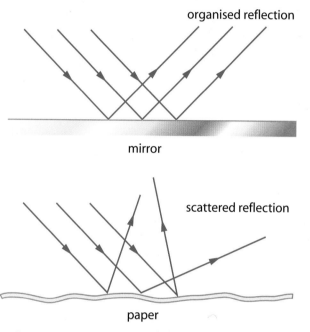

organised reflection

mirror

scattered reflection

paper

▲ Light reflecting from a mirror and light reflecting from paper

▲ The word 'ambulance' is back to front on the front of an ambulance

When you look at a poster or sign in a mirror, you'll see that the letters are back to front or **laterally inverted**. Some people wonder why the letters are back to front but not upside down. The answer is that you turned the paper back to front to show it to the mirror. If you cut the letters out so that you don't need to turn them round their reflection will be the right way round.

Interesting fact

The ancient Egyptians used mirrors to get light to the rooms inside their pyramids. The tunnels formed a maze but mirrors at each corner directed light from the Sun and then along each tunnel to the innermost tomb.

D Why is the word 'ambulance' often written back to front on the bonnet of an ambulance? (Level 6)

E (i) Which of these words is the same in mirror writing as it is in normal writing? LET, TEN, TOOT, HOOT, HANNAH.
(ii) What rules can you suggest for spotting 'mirror' words like those you identified in part (i)? (Level 7)

Keywords
angle of incidence, angle of reflection, laterally inverted, normal

Learn about:

- what happens when light travels through transparent materials
- how to draw a ray diagram to describe what happens

▲ Beware of the sharks!

One of the best attractions at a Sea Life Centre is the underwater tunnel where you can see huge stingrays and sharks swimming over you. But the question is, are they really as large as they appear? And if not, what's making them look so big?

Before we tackle this puzzle, here's another one. If you look at someone standing in a swimming pool, you can see that the person looks shorter than normal. There's something odd going on when we look at things through water, but what?

▲ Water illusions

> **A** If you look at a coin in the bottom of a swimming pool, will it look nearer or further from the surface than it really is? (Level 4)

Refraction

▲ Refraction takes place when a ray of light enters a transparent block

To investigate what's happening, take a block of clear plastic and shine a narrow beam of light into it. You can see that the beam changes direction as it goes into the block – and then changes direction again as it leaves the block.

A ray diagram shows the light's path. There are two important angles to notice – the angle of incidence and the **angle of refraction**. Look at the diagram to see how these are measured. Notice that light is bent towards the normal when it goes into the plastic. Now look at what happens when the ray leaves the plastic.

> **B** When the ray leaves the plastic, is it refracted towards the normal or away? (Level 5)

Solving the mystery

Now we can explain why people look unusually short when they stand in a swimming pool. Their feet are on the bottom of the swimming pool – at position A on the diagram. You see these feet because light shines on them and reflects back up. This light is refracted away from the normal as it leaves the water. When the light reaches your eye, your brain thinks it travelled in a straight line, from a higher position, position B in the water (see the diagram). So this is where you think the feet must be.

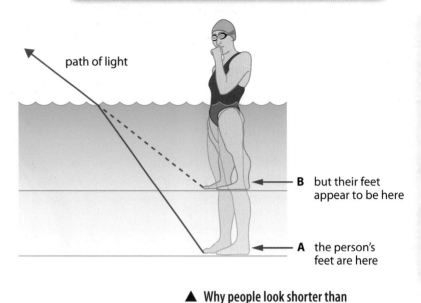

B but their feet appear to be here

A the person's feet are here

▲ Why people look shorter than usual in a swimming pool

Amazing distortions

When light travels through glass or plastic, there's even more refraction than there is in water. The table below shows the data that a scientist has collected while experimenting with light and three different materials.

The ray always begins in air and then enters the second material – which is water, glass or diamond. The table shows the angle of incidence and then the angle of refraction in the second material.

Angles of refraction in different materials

Angle of incidence in air for each experiment (°)	Experiment 1: angle of refraction in water (°)	Experiment 2: angle of refraction in glass (°)	Experiment 3: angle of refraction in diamond (°)
0	0	0	0
15	11	9	6
45	32	27	17
60	41	35	21
85	48	41	24

C Use the table to decide which of the materials tested caused the most refraction. (Level 5)

D (i) Which angle of incidence produced no refraction in any of the materials? (ii) Describe how the ray looked in this case. (Level 6)

E The largest incident angle is 85°. Why didn't the scientist try 90°? (Hint: draw a diagram to help you.) (Level 7)

Interesting fact

If you put a drop of water onto a type-written page, it magnifies the letters below it.

Keyword
angle of refraction

Learn about:

- how colours are dispersed by a prism or raindrop
- how ideas about science can change with new evidence

▲ Where do all the colours come from?

Sometimes, when you look at a CD or a plastic pen on a desk in a beam of sunlight you see a **rainbow** of colours. Where do the colours come from? The scientific answer we have today is very different from what scientists believed a few hundred years ago.

Hooke and Newton

Isaac Newton first solved the puzzle correctly. He worked out that ordinary white light contains all the colours of the rainbow. He set up a demonstration to show that his ideas were right and that another scientist, Robert Hooke, was wrong. Hooke's idea was that a prism colours the light.

Newton shone a narrow beam of ordinary light onto a prism. He saw a rainbow of colours coming from the glass. Then he blocked out all the colours except for the blue light and passed this blue light through a second prism.

If Hooke was right, the second prism would re-colour the blue light. But as Newton showed, it didn't. The blue light stayed blue. It was just as Newton demonstrated, a prism splits up the colours, and then blue light passing through a prism stays blue and red light stays red.

Newton's idea that 'light contains all the colours of the rainbow' is what we all learn at school. It is hard to imagine that scientists once doubted it. We also now know that, as Newton demonstrated, if you add together light of all the colours, the result is **white light**.

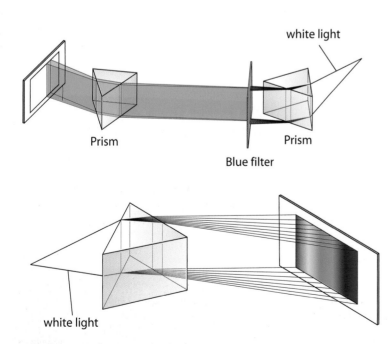

white light

Prism

Blue filter

Prism

white light

A If Hooke's explanation was correct, what would the second prism have done to the light from the first prism? (Level 4)

B Use Newton's theory of light to explain what happens when light arrives at a yellow filter. (Level 5)

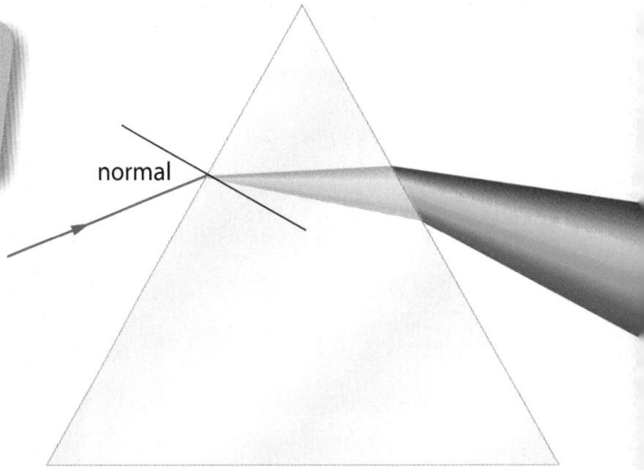

Colourful thinking

Newton's ideas changed how people thought about light. He explained where the colours of light came from and how a prism could split them up. As you can see in the diagram on the right, when sunlight falls on the prism, the rays enter the prism and are refracted towards the normal. But different colours are refracted by different amounts. The blue light is refracted most. When the light leaves the prism it is refracted away from the normal, and once again, the blue light is refracted more. Overall, this leads to **dispersal** of the colours and to a rainbow.

C Yellow light lies between red and blue on the rainbow. Is yellow light refracted more or less than red light when they pass into a prism? (Level 6)

Coloured filters

When you look at a stained glass window you see many different colours. These are all formed by the white light that shines through the glass to reach your eyes. Some colours are absorbed and others are transmitted.

Look at the picture on the right. Red glass transmits only red light and absorbs all other colours. Meanwhile the blue glass transmits only blue light and absorbs the other colours.

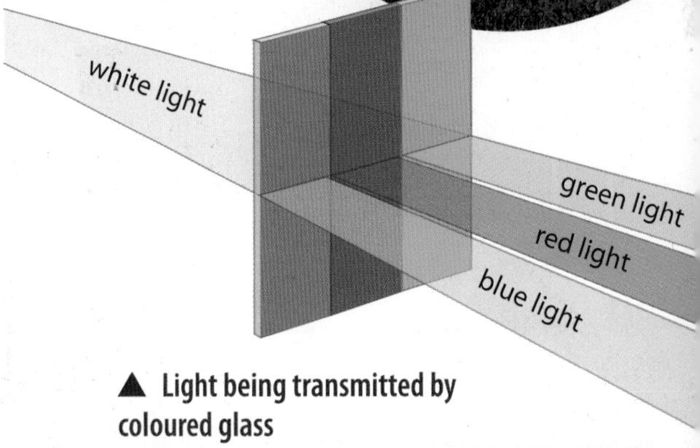

D Look again at the picture on the right. What would you see if the light shone on the window was: (i) red light? (ii) blue light? (iii) green light? (Level 6)

E Amber goes to a school disco. She is wearing a white shirt, a red skirt and black boots. What colour will her clothes be when only: (i) the red light is on? (ii) the blue light is on? (iii) the green light is on? For each answer explain why. (Level 7)

normal

▲ When light enters and leaves a glass prism, different colours are refracted by different amounts

▶ The rainbow – a case of natural and beautiful refraction

white light

green light
red light
blue light

▲ Light being transmitted by coloured glass

Interesting fact

If you look at a rainbow from a plane, you can see the rainbow going right round in a circle.

Keywords
dispersal, rainbow, white light

6.6 What's on TV?

Learn about:

- How several scientists contributed to the development of television
- How a picture reaches a television screen

Television is sometimes called our 'window to the world'. Who should we thank for this marvellous invention? Many scientists played a part, but one stands out – Scottish engineer, John Logie Baird. The dream for Baird, as well as many other scientists over 80 years ago, was to invent television.

Scientists knew how to make television work in theory – you needed a movie camera that could take pictures very fast, then you needed to get those pictures to a television screen. If the screen showed the pictures fast enough, it would look as if the things on the screen were moving. But who could make the theory work in practice?

> **A** Suppose you draw pictures of a stick man into a flick book. When you flick the pages, the man looks as if he is running. How is this similar to what is happening with a television? (Level 4)

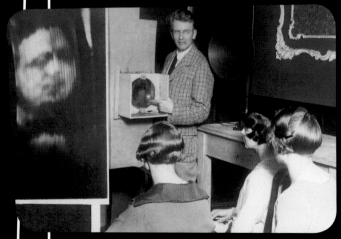

▲ Baird's television that wowed the world

The challenge of sending pictures

The tricky part of the challenge was working out how to get the photographs to the television screen. Perhaps you could use a phone line or a cable? But how can a picture travel through a cable?

Baird realised that the answer was an invention produced by a German engineering student many years before. In 1884, Paul Nipkow invented a device called the Nipkow disc.

Look at the scanned picture on the next page. It's made of coloured squares. How can you tell a friend how to draw this picture if you can only describe one square at a time? Let's say you can also say 'new line'.

You could start at the top-left square and read out the top row of colours and then say 'new line' and read out the second row. This was how Nipkow's invention worked.

The Nipkow disc has lots of holes in it. As the disc spins and each hole moves past the lens, a light cell behind the disc records the brightness of the scene row by row. This method is called scanning. It is an important step because it turns the picture into a simple code that can be sent through a wire using electricity. Once the code gets to its destination, a television turns it back into a picture.

▲ When a photo is scanned, it is turned into coloured squares or 'pixels'

B What is the role of the Nipkow disc in the television system? (Level 5)

The first Baird television

Baird made a scanner that turned a picture into 30 rows of code. Now the question was – could he send the picture to a television screen in another room? In 1926 Baird invited 50 scientists to an attic room in London to see his invention. It was called 'the Televisor'. The transmitting machine had a large disc that spun and a lens. The message was turned into an electrical signal and sent though a wire to a receiver with a screen. The picture on the screen was grey and fuzzy. But that didn't matter – it was the world's first working television. Baird had won the race!

▲ Nipkow's scanning device consisted of a huge thin disc that turned

C Describe the working steps or processes that Baird showed in his television demonstration. (Level 6)

D Most inventions are improved after their initial production. List five features that a modern television has that the Televisor did not have. (Level 7)

Interesting fact

Once Baird's Televisor was working, he asked an office boy from the next-door office to be filmed by it. Baird said 'He was the first person ever to be seen by television; but I had to bribe him with half a crown to become historical!' (John Baird, 1939)

In science, discoveries are rarely made by the work of just one scientist. Science and invention require many minds and lots of creativity. Baird's invention was only possible because of things that other scientists had developed before him, including electricity, movie cameras and Nipkow's disc. Many scientists have since built on Baird's work to give us colour televisions that can receive a signal through the air, rather than through a wire, and make it into a picture.

Learn about:

- light and how to use it to convey information
- how to detect light without your eyes
- sending a message on a light beam

Imagine that you are in a spacecraft on a mission to Mars. Your colleagues are in another spacecraft. The radio link between the two spacecraft has failed. The spacecraft are close enough so that you could wave to each other through the spacecraft windows or you could flash a light in Morse code. But wouldn't it be great if you could find some way to send your voices. In this activity you are going to put a voice on a light beam.

Best Science Lesson Ever

A Why can't you just open the spacecraft windows and shout across to each other? (Level 4)

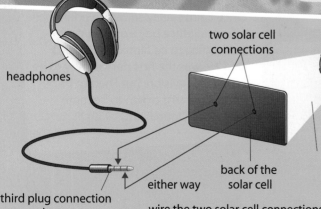

▲ How can you communicate in space?

▼ A solar cell and headphones can be used to hear light

Light beam receiver

You are going to make a simple light beam receiver. A solar cell converts light into electricity. Headphones convert electricity into sound. So if you wire the two together you can use them to 'hear' light.

Organise yourselves into groups of five. For each group, you will need:

- 2 croc-clip leads
- a solar cell
- a set of headphones
- a bright torch

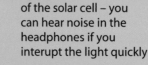

headphones

two solar cell connections

torch light

light falls on the front of the solar cell – you can hear noise in the headphones if you interupt the light quickly

third plug connection not used

either way

back of the solar cell

wire the two solar cell connections to the two end connections on the headphones plug

Use the croc-clip leads to wire the two solar cell connections to the two end connections on the headphone plug.

Then shine the torch onto the solar cell. Can you hear anything?

What happens if you flash the light by quickly waving your hand between the torch and the receiver?

98

B Can you hear the light beam from the torch when the light is steady? (Level 5)

C Explain how and why you can use the light beam receiver to 'hear' the invisible beam from a TV remote control. (Level 6)

Light beam transmitter

Now you are going to make a simple light beam transmitter. For each group, you will need:

- a cardboard tube
- aluminium foil or a balloon and a small mirror
- a torch

Interesting fact

Your eyes only see a narrow range of the light that is out there. With the light beam receiver you can 'hear' more than you can see.

Fix a piece of aluminium foil to the end of the cardboard tube with the shiny side outwards.

Now talk into the tube. If you gently touch the foil you can feel that the sound of your voice transfers to the foil causing it to vibrate.

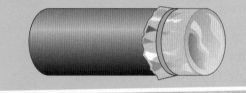

Shine the torch on the foil, the reflected spot of light will dart about a little due to these vibrations. This is because the brightness (amplitude) is changing very quickly.

Sending a message

Now you can use your light beam transmitter and light beam receiver to send a message. Shine your torch onto the foil on the light beam transmitter and talk into the tube. Position the solar cell of your light beam receiver so that the reflected light beam is sent to it. You will only hear something when the light moves or changes brightness

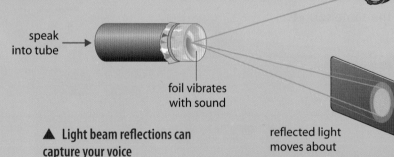

torch light

speak into tube →

foil vibrates with sound

▲ Light beam reflections can capture your voice

reflected light moves about

Written by Jonathan Hare, co-presenter BBC's Rough Science series

If you did this from one spacecraft to the other and it was very quiet, you could communicate in this way. To get this to work in the classroom, your teacher will need to give you a simple pre-amp to boost the signals. With this and a bit of experimentation, you will hear your voice being sent by light beam communication.

D Explain what a pre-amp does and how it might help our light beam communications. (Level 7)

Nails on a blackboard? A dentist's drill? A screaming baby? Scientists wanted to know what sound people found most unpleasant. How did they do it? How would you do it?

Acoustic engineers at the University of Salford recorded dozens of hideous sounds. They put them on a website and asked visitors to rate the unpleasantness of each. Over a million people completed the survey.

And the results showed that the worst sound of all was … the sound of someone vomiting. The project was designed by Professor Trevor Cox of the University's Acoustic Research Centre. 'The aim was to find out what makes a sound unpleasant to hear.'

Using the Internet made it easy to find participants, but the disadvantages with this method were that people were not sampled randomly and they listened to the sounds through their computers and so did not hear exactly the same sounds.

Now try these

- How is energy transferred when a guitar is played?

- The acoustic engineers at Salford University compared the responses from men and women. What other comparisons would be interesting, and why?

- If the skin of a drum is tightened, it vibrates more quickly. How does this change the note of the drum?

Coming up in this Section ...

usical instruments produce rations that last a long time

Ear protection is worn by people who work in noisy places

Foam in a studio absorbs sound to stop echoes

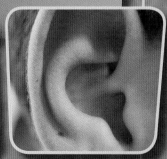

Your ear catches vibrations and directs them into your head

▶ Can an opera singer break a glass using only their voice?

Learn about:

- how sounds are made
- the importance of fairness and safety when doing an investigation
- whether a singer's voice can smash a glass

It's said that an opera singer can smash a wine glass just by singing the right note – but is it true?

It sounds possible, when you think about how sounds are made.

> When an instrument vibrates, it makes a sound. But why is there a sound when you knock on a table – a table can't vibrate – can it?

> When I pluck a guitar string, I can feel it vibrating.

It's not just musical instruments that vibrate to produce sounds. If you tap a door, a cup, a radiator or even a table, they also vibrate. Musical instruments are designed to vibrate for a long time to make a sound that lasts. The vibrations in everyday objects usually fade away quickly. The **pitch** of the note, how high or low it sounds, depends on the number of vibrations that happen each second. This is called the **frequency** of the vibrations.

A model to explain how sounds reach your ears

When something vibrates, it repeatedly knocks the air particles around it – and they begin to vibrate. These particles in turn knock the particles next to them. Movement energy is passed from one particle to the next. When the vibrations reach your ear, they are converted to electrical messages which are sent to the brain. Your brain interprets these as a sound.

▲ This is another way to imagine how sound travels using the model of sound as a wave. When you toss a stone into a pond, waves of water move out across the pond. Waves transfer the energy across the pond

 A Which of these are forms of energy: light, sound, movement? (Level 4)

Amplification

The vibrating prongs of a tuning fork produce a soft sound. But if you stand the tuning fork on a desk, the sound becomes louder. This is because the desk is now being forced to vibrate at the same frequency as the tuning fork. This **amplifies**, or in other words, increases the sound.

B Why does an electrical buzzer sound louder if you hold it against a polystyrene cup? (Level 5)

Most musical instruments have a sound box as part of the instrument to amplify the sound. When playing a guitar, the wooden body of the guitar amplifies the sound of the vibrating strings.

C If you put your hand on the body of a violin while it is being played, what might you feel and why? (Level 5)

Scientists at work

Windows let in lots of noise from outside. Curtains and double glazing help a bit, but something better is on the way. Scientists are hoping that one day we will have anti-noise windows to cancel out any sounds coming in.

Resonance

Sometimes, when a truck goes by, your windows rattle. It's an example of **resonance**. The vibrations from the truck travel through the air and ground and vibrate the objects they reach. If the glass panes vibrate naturally at the frequency of vibrations produced by the truck then the panes will vibrate strongly as the truck passes.

D Based on what you've read, how would you explain resonance? (Level 6)

The shattering glass

So could a singer shatter a glass just by singing the right note? Scientists say it's a difficult theory to test. The problem is that if the singer is far from the glass, the vibrations are too weak by the time they reach the glass. If the singer puts their mouth near the glass, shards of glass may strike them.

▲ Testing the theory safely

E In an experiment, a singer stands behind a plastic screen for protection and tries to break a wine glass on the other side with their voice. (i) What's wrong with this technique? (ii) Would a jet of air blowing the broken glass away from their face do the trick? (Level 7)

Keywords
amplify, frequency, pitch, resonance

But here's a safer way to test the theory. Scientists put a speaker close to a glass playing the singer's voice. They turned the volume right up – and a moment later, the glass smashed.

Learn about:

- how sound travels in different materials
- how a fingerphone produces a sound
- considering evidence to support ideas

▲ The fingerphone – a ring that turns your finger into a phone

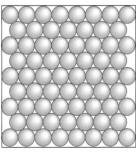

In a solid each particle touches many other particles. It is very easy to pass the energy from particle to particle.

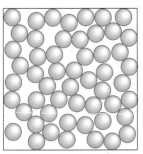

In a liquid the particles are touching, but each particle has fewer neighbours. This means that the energy is passed on less easily.

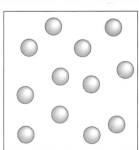

In a gas the particles are far apart. It is more difficult to pass the energy from particle to particle.

In a vacuum there are no particles. The energy cannot be passed on or transferred.

Quick – your finger is ringing! Right now, if you own a mobile phone, the chances are that it has a speaker to produce the sound. The speaker vibrates, vibrating the air around it, and these vibrations are carried to your eardrum for you to hear. But it doesn't have to be this way.

Sound vibrations don't only travel through air. In fact, they travel better through many other materials. If you put your hand over your ear and tap your elbow, you can hear vibrations that have travelled through the bones in your arm to your ear. There is now a phone that uses this idea. You wear the phone like a ring and it transmits sound vibrations along your finger bone directly into your ear. You put a finger in your ear to hear them.

Why sound travels faster through solid materials

Sound vibrations travel through solids faster and with less loss than through gases. This is because energy is transferred more easily in a denser material. In a **vacuum**, like Space, there are no particles and sound vibrations cannot be transferred at all. That's why it's true to say that in Space 'no one can hear you scream'!

A If you tap on a table, the sound travels faster through the wood than through the air – true or false? (Level 4)

B Explain in your own words why sounds cannot travel through a vacuum. (Level 5)

Bell? I hear no bell

The first scientist to show that sound cannot travel through a vacuum was Robert Boyle in 1660. He put a small bell into an airtight jar. By turning a handle outside the jar, Boyle could make a striker strike the bell. He turned the handle and everyone heard the bell ring.

Then Boyle pumped the air out of the jar. When there was no air around the bell, he turned the handle again. The vibrations could no longer travel away from the bell, so as far as Boyle's audience were concerned, the bell was silent.

C Boyle's experiment has been repeated with a ringing alarm clock. The sound of the clock fades to nothing as the air is removed. Why? (Level 6)

▲ Boyle astonished his fellow scientists with his demonstration of a silent ringing bell

Sounding good

The table below shows the speed of sound in different materials. In most cases, the denser the material, the faster the speed.

The speed of sound in different materials		
Material	**Description**	**Speed of sound (m/s)**
air	gas	330
water	liquid	1500
wood (oak)	solid	3850
iron	solid	5000

Use the data in the table to answer the following questions.

D Jon says a sound travels five times faster through water than through air. Kate says it will travel twice as fast through air. Who is right? (Level 6)

E Sara swims underwater at the swimming pool and is surprised at how loud everything sounds down there. Explain why this is, using the ideas on these pages. (Level 7)

Interesting fact

When a mother elephant sends a distress signal to the herd, she stamps her feet to produce low frequency vibrations in the ground. These vibrations travel huge distances – and are picked up by other elephants with their feet.

▲ An elephant sending a distress signal

Keyword
vacuum

Learn about:

- high- and low-pitched notes
- ways to represent a sound visually
- how scientific experiments and instruments can help test everyday beliefs

Can a duck's quack echo? There's a widespread myth that it never can. Scientists at the University of Salford found this puzzling, seeing no scientific reason why it wouldn't. These scientists were acoustic engineers – scientists who study sound.

Down by the river

Down at a noisy river, it's difficult to tell whether the quacks of ducks are echoing or not. So to test out the theory, the engineers put a single duck, Daisy, into a specially designed padded chamber that produces no echoes, called an **anechoic chamber**. They recorded a single quack.

Then they put her into an **echoic chamber** – which is a room with bare walls that reflects sounds much like a cathedral does. How would the two recordings compare?

> After looking at the evidence, it's clear that a duck's quack can definitely echo.

 A Did the engineers at Salford predict that there would or would not be an echo in the echoic chamber? (Level 4)

B Why was it useful to record a single quack in the padded chamber first? (Level 5)

A single quack

The diagram shows a visual display of Daisy's quack in each location. It shows how the **amplitude** or volume of the recording changes in time. You can see that in the anechoic chamber, there is a long croaky quack that finishes abruptly. But in the echoic (echoey) chamber, the sound builds up to a continuous blur of loud sound and then fades away slowly as it echoes around the room.

anechoic

echoic

▲ The quack recorded in the anechoic chamber and the quack recorded in the echoic chamber

Perfect pitch

Scientists use instruments to see both the amplitude and also the pitch of sounds. The pitch or **frequency** of a note depends on the number of vibrations per second. Suppose a guitar string vibrates at 500 vibrations per second, we write this as a frequency of 500 **Hertz** or 500 **Hz**.

 C A string vibrates at 400 Hz. How many times does it vibrate in 1 second? (Level 5)

Seeing sounds

An **oscilloscope** is an electrical device with a microphone, a display and a speaker. It converts sound, that we can't see, into an image on the screen that we can see. It is a good instrument to use when investigating pitch. Musical instruments produce many notes at the same time, which makes it difficult to see what's going on. But we can set the oscilloscope's speaker to vibrate at 500 Hz and so produce a pure tone.

Sound waves

As the speaker vibrates, the air around it vibrates. The particles of air transfer on their sound energy (vibrations) to particles around them. The sound energy eventually reaches the air around the oscilloscope's microphone. The display represents the energy as a wave. Since the speaker is vibrating all the time, this happens again and again, which is why you see a repeated pattern of waves on the display.

D How many sound waves does a speaker playing a note of 500 Hz produce in a second? (Level 6)

E The oscilloscope in the picture below is displaying the sound waves it detects when the speaker vibrates at 500 Hz. How many seconds are shown on the screen? (Level 7)

A higher note

If you raise the pitch of the note, the oscilloscope display shows that there are more waves in the same amount of time. If you continue to raise the pitch, the waves become more and more compressed. Eventually they go beyond the limit of human hearing – which occurs at about 20 000 Hz in children.

▲ Sound energy is transferred by vibrations

▼ This note has a frequency of 500 Hz. The screen shows two complete waves

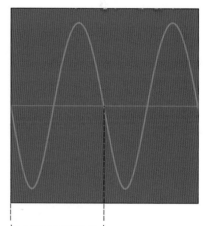

one complete wave or vibration

Foul Fact

Our vocal cords vibrate to make sound. Smokers often have deep gravelly voices because smoking causes the vocal cords to thicken with mucus.

Keywords
amplitude, anechoic chamber, echoic chamber, frequency, Hertz (Hz), oscilloscope

one complete wave or vibration

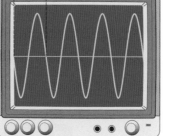

▲ This note has a higher frequency than the one above

The bionic ear

Learn about:

- how we hear
- how the bionic ear has helped some people to hear

Graeme Clark's father was deaf and Graeme wanted to help him hear. He became a researcher at Melbourne University, Australia, and started work on a bionic ear – a device that could pick up sound waves and turn them into a signal the brain would understand.

The bionic ear

Professor Graeme Clark's finished invention came too late to help his father, but it has helped thousands of others around the world to hear, including children like Callum. He was born deaf, and didn't hear his mother speak until the day his bionic ear was switched on.

How we hear sound

For you to hear a sound, first something has to make a sound, then your ear has to detect it, and then your brain has to interpret the signal as a sound. Here's how it happens.

1. Sound waves – which are vibrating air particles – enter the ear and move down the **ear canal** to the **eardrum**.
2. The eardrum vibrates and this causes three tiny bones behind the drum to vibrate as well.
3. A fluid in a container called the **cochlea**, deep inside the ear, begins to vibrate. Tiny hairs inside the cochlea sway to the vibrations.
4. These hairs produce electrical signals which travel through a nerve to the brain. Inside the brain, the electrical signals are interpreted as sounds.

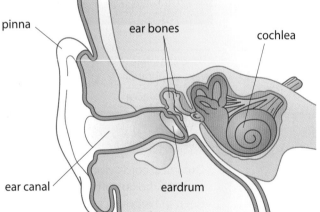

▲ How we hear a sound

A Use the information above to explain how earplugs reduce the noise you hear. (Level 4)

B A burst or torn eardrum is very painful. Why does it also affect hearing? (Level 5)

C The hair cells inside the cochlea are fragile and if they die, they never repair. Why are people who listen to loud music on headphones in danger of losing their hearing? (Level 6)

What can go wrong?

For some deaf people, the cause of their deafness is that the cochlea is not working. The bionic ear has a microphone to pick up sound vibrations and an artificial cochlea to transfer vibrations into electrical signals. These signals are then sent along the nerve to the brain. Once the device is fitted, the wearer's brain learns to interpret these signals as sound.

D Fill in the missing words. The artificial cochlea transfers energy from _____ to _____ . (Level 6)

Frequency range

Most people can detect thousands of different frequencies. The hairs inside the cochlea are different lengths. Each length responds to a different pitch, and this is how our brains tell different sounds apart. The bionic ear currently only detects a few frequencies of sound, but it's enough to help the wearer understand speech.

A secret tone

How well you hear depends on many factors including your age and whether you take care of your hearing. A young healthy person can hear frequencies from about 20 to 20 000 Hz. As they get older, most people can no longer hear the highest pitched sounds. Some companies now produce mobile phones with ring tones that only young people can hear.

E A recent news story said that some shopkeepers were using squealing devices to drive young people off their premises. Older people weren't affected. How might these devices work? (Level 7)

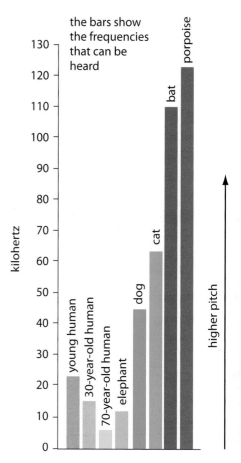

▲ Hearing loss from age 10 to 80 in humans compared to some animals

▲ Bats and dolphins can hear ultrasonic (very high) frequencies beyond the range of human hearing

Keywords
cochlea, ear canal, eardrum

Highest audible frequency for selected species	
Species	Highest audible frequency (Hz)
human	20 000
dog	45 000
bat	120 000
dolphin	200 000

6.13 The noisiest city in Britain?

earn about:

- how sounds are measured
- why some sounds can damage your hearing

Newcastle is the noisiest city in Britain according to a survey of 41 towns and cities around the country. Researchers from University College London measured traffic noise during rush hour periods. They took several readings at each site so that unusually loud sounds would not overly influence the result. The researchers concluded that the roar of traffic in Newcastle is equivalent to having a loud alarm clock constantly ringing in your ears.

When there's a hideous whine … or a horrible hum … who ya gonna call? The noise busters!

As an acoustic engineer, you could find yourself working on all kinds of projects – from how to cut traffic noise in a city, to using a computer to model the sounds on a new construction site.

Road wars

Traffic noise is a problem for lots of people. It keeps them awake and drowns out TV, music and conversation. A recent study by scientists at a London University pointed out just how bad the noise can get.

cientists at work

A sound meter is a device that engineers use to measure the loudness of a sound in decibels. By law, anyone who works with a daily noise level at or above 85 decibels must wear ear protection.

A How did the researchers ensure that one-off loud sounds at the roadside did not distort their results? (Level 4)

B Why did the researchers measure the traffic noise at rush hour rather than at other times during the day? (Level 5)

C At what times of day would loud traffic noise upset people the most? (Level 6)

But was the study fair?

When this study was reported in the press, some people complained. They said that the researchers picked on a particularly noisy spot to make their measurements and the press then implied that the whole of Newcastle is noisy.

And what can be done?

To reduce traffic noise, engineers advise road builders to use a rubberised asphalt road surface and to dig a valley for the road so that it is surrounded by banks. Roadside barriers are another option.

> **D** Why is the headline 'Newcastle is the noisiest city' not a fair report of the scientists' study? (Level 6)

▲ Building barriers and recessing roads help to reduce traffic noise

Keeping up with the jargon

One of the most important terms in the engineer's phrase book is the **decibel**. This is the unit that describes the loudness of a sound. The term 'bel' was chosen as a tribute to Alexander Graham Bell, who invented the telephone.

The decibel scale is peculiar because as you go up the scale, each step represents a bigger and bigger jump in volume. So for very loud sounds, a tiny increase in the decibel reading indicates a huge increase in volume.

The loudness of different sounds

Sound	Sound level in decibels (dB)
the quietest sound that humans can hear	0
whisper	30
chatting	60
traffic noise in noisiest cities	80
thunderclap	110
explosion	120

Another important idea is that the loudness of a sound when it reaches someone's ear depends on the distance to the source of the sound as well as the volume of the sound at its source. So a vacuum cleaner close to your ear sounds noisier than a jet plane hundreds of miles away.

> **E** Ryan is editing music in a studio but is bothered by a roadside drill and a whirring printer. The printer bothers him more. Why? (Level 7)

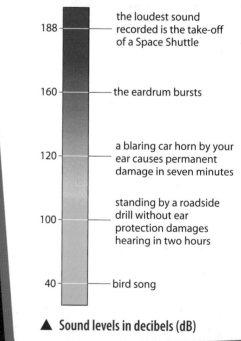

188	the loudest sound recorded is the take-off of a Space Shuttle
160	the eardrum bursts
120	a blaring car horn by your ear causes permanent damage in seven minutes
100	standing by a roadside drill without ear protection damages hearing in two hours
40	bird song

▲ Sound levels in decibels (dB)

Painfully loud

How loud does a sound have to be to damage your hearing? Once a sound gets above 90 decibels it's likely to cause permanent damage. But there's another factor as well as the loudness of the sound – and that's how long you listen to the sound for.

Keyword
decibel

Assess your progress

Level 4

1 Name two luminous objects.

2 Mark sees a rainbow of colours on a CD which is lit by his bedroom light. Where have the colours come from?

3 Look at page 97. Could Baird's Televisor have been invented before electricity was discovered?

4 The thinnest guitar string produces a higher-pitched note than the fattest string. Is it vibrating more quickly or more slowly?

5 Put these sounds in order of loudness:

car horn   space shuttle take-off   vacuum cleaner   whisper

Level 5

6 Use the particle model to explain why a white car looks white.

7 If you reflect a word in a mirror and then reflect it in a second mirror, will it still be laterally inverted?

8 Look at the table on page 93 showing different angles of incidence. Does glass always produce more refraction than water for rays travelling from air?

9 Tanya operates the stage lighting for a theatre. She has lights of every colour, but not white. If she points all the coloured lights at the stage, could she produce a white spotlight?

10 Dean plucks a guitar string and notices that he can hear the note for several seconds. What is happening during this time?

11 If a string vibrates for two seconds at 500 Hz and is then stopped, how many times does it vibrate?

12 The hairs in the cochlea are fragile. If you permanently damage them by listening to loud music, how will this affect your hearing?

Level 6

13 Use the particle model to explain why a black snake looks black.

14 Jeff has a mysterious transparent cube. He shines a ray of light onto it at an angle of 45°. He measures an angle of refraction of 25°. What might the cube be made from? Use the table on page 93 to help you decide.

15 Jo makes a rainbow by spraying water into the air on a sunny day. Lara looks through the water, facing the Sun, hoping to see the rainbow. How can she improve her chances?

16 Why is it helpful to stand a tuning fork on a desk if you want to hear the sound clearly?

17 An alien planet has an atmosphere of helium. Do sounds travel through the alien atmosphere faster or more slowly than here on Earth?

18 Use the table on page 109 to explain why a dog whistle is audible to dogs but not humans.

19 Why are workmen who use road drills more likely than passers-by to suffer hearing damage if they don't wear ear protection? Give two reasons.

Level 7

20 If you increase the angle of incidence of a ray by 20°, how does this change the angle between the incident and reflected rays?

21 People sometimes jump into deep water thinking they will be able to stand on the bottom with their head above water. Use your understanding of the refraction of light to explain why they think this.

22 Use the comparison of ripples on a pond to explain how a sound travels through air.

23 The height of a wave on an oscilloscope indicates the amplitude of the sound. Copy the drawing of an oscilloscope on page 107. Draw in a sound wave, then draw a second wave corresponding to a softer sound of the same frequency. Label them both.

24 In a science lab tank, a speaker and microphone are placed 2.6 metres apart. The space between them is filled with oil. How long will a sound take to travel from the speaker to the microphone approximately?

We now know that the Earth has a magnetic field. But it has not been easy for scientists to learn about it. Before Space travel was possible, scientists could not go into Space to investigate the Earth's magnetic field. So they used models to explore what it looked like and its properties.

They discovered that the Earth has an iron core which produces its magnetic field. They couldn't do experiments on the Earth's core. So ideas about why some pieces of iron are magnetic and some are not had to be tested by doing experiments in the laboratory. Scientists also collected lots of data and evidence from rocks about the magnetic history of the Earth, which they analysed. They drew conclusions based on the evidence and then evaluated these conclusions.

Investigations into the Earth's magnetic field are still going on. Scientists all over the world in all fields of scientific research use the scientific skills of modelling, experimenting, collecting data and evidence, and making and evaluating conclusions. They are the same skills that you use when you do science at school.

Now try these

- List as many objects as you can that use magnets or magnetism.

- Suggest how a satellite could find out if the Moon had a magnetic field.

- If the Earth has a magnetic field that acts like the field of a bar magnet, what shape will this field be?

Coming up in this Chapter ...

...ny magnets in volcanic rocks tell ...entists about Earth's history

Computers use magnets to store information on their hard drives

This electromagnet lifts scrap metal

Birds use magnetism to navigate over vast distances

Learn about:

- how science has its roots in different cultures
- what makes a magnet and how they are used

▶ This ancient compass pointed the way for sailors

People have known about **magnets** and **magnetism** for centuries. It is thought that an ancient Greek philosopher called Thales made the first observations on magnetism 2500 years ago. But it wasn't until the beginning of the seventeenth century that scientists began to really understand how magnetism works.

We have used magnets for a very long time. Chinese and Viking sailors used a special type of magnetic stone as a compass to help them navigate their sailing ships over 1000 years ago. Nowadays, you may use a debit card to pay for your school meals, and use computers for work and play. They both contain magnets.

Magnetism is a very useful property that only a few substances have. The only magnetic materials are **iron**, **steel**, **cobalt** and **nickel**. Magnetism is a force that acts at a distance.

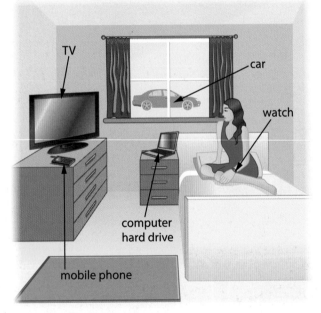

▲ Magnets are used all around the home. Your life would be very different without them

A Which of the following metals cannot be used as a compass? (Level 4)
iron   aluminium   cobalt   copper

B Why would you think that a piece of stone was magnetic? (Level 5)

north pole   south pole

| N | S |

▲ A bar magnet

Magnetism

Look at the drawing of a bar magnet. It has a **north pole** at one end and a **south pole** at the other.

If you bring the poles of two bar magnets together:

- if the poles are the same, the magnets will repel each other
- if the poles are opposite, the magnets will attract each other.

What makes iron magnetic?

Some pieces of iron behave as magnets and others do not. Why is this? Magnetic materials are made up of tiny magnets. We can model these tiny magnets as straight needles, like the needle on a compass.

In an ordinary bar of iron, all these magnets point in different directions. Their magnetism is cancelled out because for every magnet pointing one way, there is a magnet pointing the other. But if most of these tiny magnets are pointing in the same direction, the iron bar becomes magnetic.

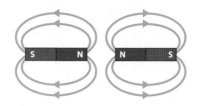

▲ What happens when two poles of a magnet come together

▼ Lined-up magnets make an iron bar a magnet

unmagnetised

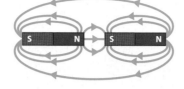

magnetised

C What do you think is the relationship between the number of tiny magnets pointing in the same direction and the strength of a magnet? (Level 6)

Making a magnet

A non-magnetic iron nail can be magnetised with a magnet. All you need to do is stroke the magnet along the nail. As you drag the magnet along the nail, it will make all the north poles turn and point one way and all the south poles point the other way. You can see this in the diagram.

▲ Making an iron nail magnetic

D Ryan says that because his magnet is bigger than Sam's it must be stronger. Is he correct? Explain your answer. (Level 7)

Magnetic money

George is a bank manager. He says 'Debit cards are just like carrying money in your pocket. The magnetic strip along the back keeps a lot of information on it. The strip is made of little magnets, lined up in different ways. Different patterns of poles stand for different letters and numbers.'

4977 1236 9674

▲ The magnetic code on the magnetic strip

▲ You can only buy things with a debit card if you know your code number

E Explain why it might be a problem if you bring a powerful magnet near a debit card. (Level 7)

Keywords
cobalt, iron, magnet, magnetism, nickel, north pole, south pole, steel

7.3 Magnetic protection

Learn about:

- what magnetic fields are and their shapes
- how the Earth's magnetic field was discovered and why it is important

▲ The Northern Lights

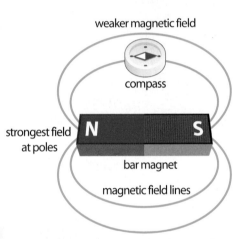

weaker magnetic field

compass

strongest field at poles

N   S

bar magnet

magnetic field lines

▲ How you can test the shape and strength of a magnetic field

The Sun gives us the light and heat we need for life. It also sends radiation that would kill all life on Earth. The Northern Lights are a sign that the Earth is protecting us from the dangerous radiation from the Sun. The Earth can do this because it has a **magnetic field** around it.

What is a magnetic field?

When scientists say that there is a magnetic field around a magnet, they mean that there is an area around it where the magnet will affect magnetic materials. Any object that contains iron, steel, nickel or cobalt will be attracted to a magnet if it is in its field.

You can test this using a compass. It shows you the shape and strength of the magnet's field. The diagram shows the magnetic field around a bar magnet. Scientists call the lines on the diagram **magnetic field lines**.

Science to the rescue

Doctors put people with serious illnesses inside a magnetic field to look inside their bodies without cutting them open. This is called an MRI scan.

A What could the compass needle be made of? (Level 4)

B Suggest how can you tell from the diagram that the field is strongest at the poles? (Level 5)

How the Earth's magnetic field was discovered

In the sixteenth century William Gilbert first suggested that the Earth had a magnetic field around it. This was hundreds of years before we sent objects into space. He did it by modelling the Earth. He made a small magnetic ball and did experiments with it using a compass. The compass behaved near the model like it did on the Earth. William decided that this meant the Earth was magnetic.

Gilbert found that the needle dipped at different angles depending on how far north or south you were. These discoveries led to an instrument being made to help sailors find out their position at sea.

William Gilbert was one of the first scientists to gather a team of experts to help make discoveries and inventions. A compass maker noticed that the needle in his compass dipped towards the ground as well as pointing north.

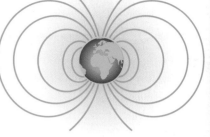

▲ The shape of the Earth's magnetic field

C Apart from being magnetic, in what other way is Gilbert's model like the Earth? (Level 5)

D Sailors used to work out how far north or south they were by using stars and the Sun. What was the advantage of William Gilbert's invention? (Level 6)

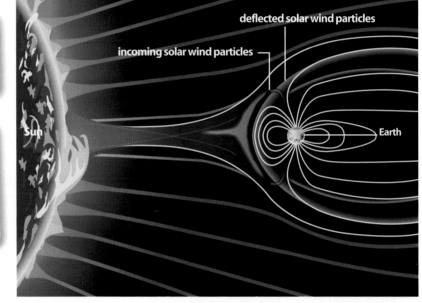

deflected solar wind particles

incoming solar wind particles

Sun

Earth

▲ How the Earth's magnetic field deflects radiation

How the Earth's magnetic field protects us

The Sun produces something called the solar wind. This is a stream of deadly particles. When these reach the Earth they travel along the Earth's magnetic field lines to the poles. Here the energy is transferred into light – the Northern Lights.

Does the Sun have a magnetic field?

In science, we look for patterns. If two things behave in the same way or look similar, then it might be because the same thing is happening.

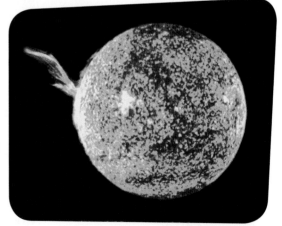

▶ A solar flare

E Take a look at the photo of the solar flare. How can you tell from the photo that the Sun may have a magnetic field? (Level 7)

Keywords
magnetic field, magnetic field lines

119

Learn about:

- how electromagnets work and what they are used for
- how to analyse what affects their strength

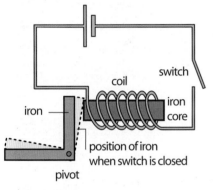

A simple electromagnet

▲ Magnets are used in recycling plants

Sometimes you want to be able to turn a magnet on and off. You need an **electromagnet**. Graham is the manager of a recycling plant. 'In the recycling plant the magnet is turned on to separate the steel cans from the aluminium cans. When you want to take the steel cans away you turn the electromagnet off and they fall into a skip,' he says.

> **A** Why can a magnet separate steel cans from aluminium cans? (Level 4)

How an electromagnet works

An electromagnet is made by using electricity to make a piece of iron magnetic. When a wire has an electric current running through it, the current creates a magnetic field. If you twist the wire into a coil, the magnetic field has the same shape as a bar magnet. A piece of iron in the core makes this core field stronger.

When you close the switch:

1 an electric current goes through the wire coil
2 this makes the piece of iron inside the coil (called the core) magnetic
3 which attracts something made of iron, or any other magnetic material.

When the switch is opened, the current stops going through the wire coil and the iron core stops being magnetic. You can see how a simple electromagnet works in the diagram. All electromagnets work in the same way.

Analysing the strength of an electromagnet

Ryan and Becca are experimenting to find what affects the strength of an electromagnet. They have built a simple electromagnet and are lifting steel paperclips to measure its strength.

> First we changed the number of turns on the coil but kept the current the same. The table on the next page shows our results.

Varying the number of turns					
Number of turns	10	20	30	40	50
Paperclips lifted	3	9	16	31	40

▼ Electromagnets are strong and can hold large weights

B Look at Ryan's data table. As the number of turns increases, what happens to the strength of the magnet? (Level 4)

We then kept the number of turns the same but varied the size of the current. We made a graph of our results.

Take a look at the graph showing the size of current and number of paperclips lifted. You can see that as the current increases, so does the strength of the electromagnet.

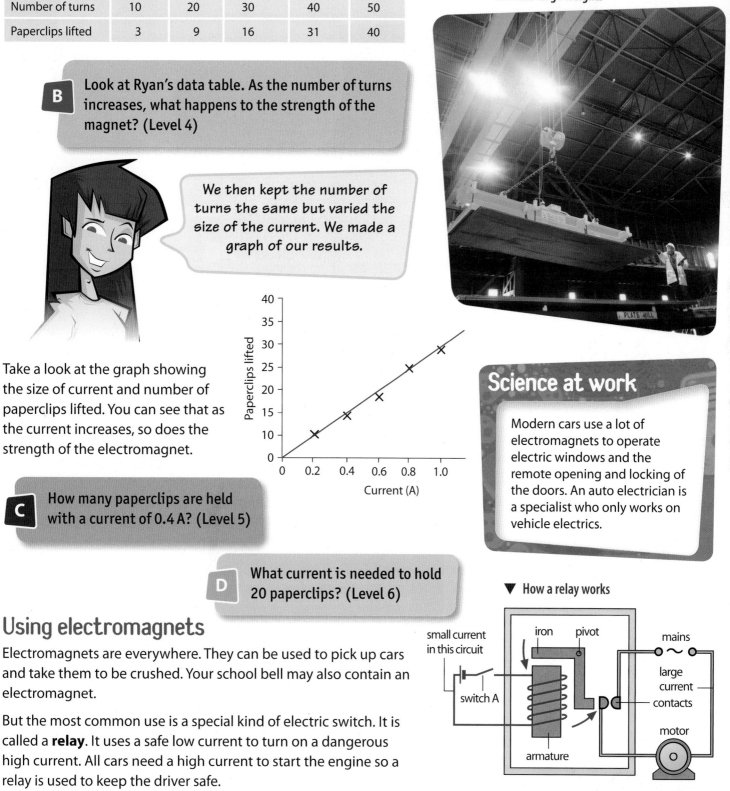

C How many paperclips are held with a current of 0.4 A? (Level 5)

Science at work

Modern cars use a lot of electromagnets to operate electric windows and the remote opening and locking of the doors. An auto electrician is a specialist who only works on vehicle electrics.

D What current is needed to hold 20 paperclips? (Level 6)

Using electromagnets

Electromagnets are everywhere. They can be used to pick up cars and take them to be crushed. Your school bell may also contain an electromagnet.

But the most common use is a special kind of electric switch. It is called a **relay**. It uses a safe low current to turn on a dangerous high current. All cars need a high current to start the engine so a relay is used to keep the driver safe.

▼ How a relay works

E Look at the diagram. Explain in detail why closing switch A makes the starter motor turn. (Level 7)

Keywords
electromagnet, relay

121

7.5 Flipping poles

Learn about:

● analysing evidence
● applying knowledge to predict the future

S

N

▲ What is wrong with the poles on this Earth?

Have a close look at the picture of the Earth. Notice anything wrong with it?

The picture may look wrong to us today but many times in the past the North and South Poles have been reversed. Scientists know this has happened in the past because they have analysed rocks from under the sea. They can also use this evidence from the rocks to predict the future.

The rocks tell the story

Look carefully at the diagram of the Mid-Atlantic ridge. Can you see a pattern between the west coast of Africa and the east coast of South America? They look like two pieces of a jigsaw that should go together.

They were joined together in the past and have been moving apart for millions of years. Half-way between them is a very deep ocean basin. New rock is made at a ridge in the middle of the basin, it comes from inside the Earth. The plates are being moved by convection currents within the Earth, so a gap opens at the ridge. The gap is filled with new rock, as a result the continents are slowly moving further apart.

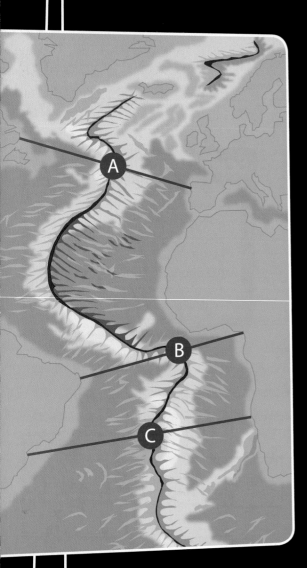

▲ The Mid-Atlantic ridge

A Measure the distance from points A, B and C to each coast on the diagram of the Mid-Atlantic ridge. What pattern do you find? (Level 4)

B Does the result support the theory that new rock is pushing the continents apart? Explain your answer. (Level 5)

Magnetic rocks

When the rocks come to the surface of the seabed, they have small magnetic crystals in them. Before the new rock becomes solid these crystals line up with the Earth's magnetic field. The north-seeking poles point north. The diagram shows what the scientists found when they used a magnetometer at different distances on the sea bed.

Every few hundred thousand years, the crystal magnets change direction. The crystals cannot move once the rock is solid. This evidence tells scientists that the North and South Poles of the Earth swap over every few hundred thousand years.

▲ New rock comes to the surface in the Mid-Atlantic ridge

C Look at the diagram showing the magnetic patterns in the rock. How often have the poles flipped in about a million years? (Level 5)

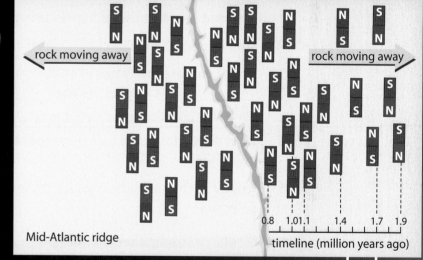

rock moving away → rock moving away

Mid-Atlantic ridge

0.8 1.0 1.1 1.4 1.7 1.9
timeline (million years ago)

▲ The magnetic patterns in the rock

D Suggest why an earthquake underground can't explain the crystal magnets pointing in different ways. (Level 6)

What will happen when the North and South Poles change again?

You may have realised that the poles are due to change places again. We do not know exactly when this will happen but it will cause a lot of problems. The most obvious problem is that all compasses will point the wrong way. Also, satellites use the Earth's magnetic field to line themselves up in the correct place. They could end up crashing back to Earth. Animals and birds are also thought to use magnetism when they migrate so they could end up in the wrong place.

E Scientists have found evidence that the magnetic field around the Earth shuts off for a time before the poles swap places. Why might this be dangerous to life on Earth? (Level 7)

Assess your progress

Level 4

1. You take a bar magnet and cut it in two. Draw the two magnets, labelling the poles on each of the new magnets.

2. Copy and complete the sentences using some of the words below:

   ends   force   stronger   magnetic   poles   weaker

   The area surrounding a magnet is called its _____ field. The _____ the magnet, the larger its field. The field is strongest at the north and south _____.

3. Copy and complete the sentences using some of the words below:

   aluminium   coil   core   iron   current   attract   repel

   When you close the switch of an electromagnet a _____ flows through the _____. This magnetises the _____. This would _____ something that is made of _____.

4. What do you think will happen to the strength of an electromagnet if you use a thicker iron core?

5. Why don't the magnetic crystals in the rocks under the sea change direction when the poles flip?

Level 5

6. You bring two iron bars together and they attract each other. You then turn one of the bars round and bring them together again. They still attract each other. What does this tell you about each of the bars?

7. If you place a piece of iron on top of a table and move a magnet under it, the iron follows the magnet. What does this tell you about magnetic fields?

8. Look at Ryan's data table on page 123 which shows the number of turns on the coil and the number of paperclips picked up. Use the data to produce a graph. How many paperclips would be held if the coil had 35 turns?

9. Look at the diagram on page 123 of the poles flipping. How long has it been since the poles last swapped places?

Level 6

10 Look at the diagram of the poles flipping. Using the scale shown, note down the times between the poles flipping. Work out the average time.

11 You can destroy a magnet by heating it up. Why do you think this is? Explain your answer.

12 The Earth has a magnetic field. What might this tell you about the inside of the Earth?

13 If you pass a current along a coil wrapped around a steel core it will become permanently magnetic. Explain why this is a problem if you use the steel core in an electromagnet.

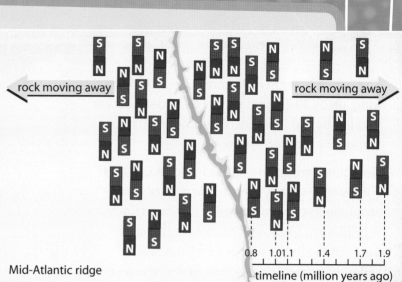

▲ The magnetic patterns in the rock

rock moving away   rock moving away

0.8 1.0 1.1   1.4   1.7 1.9

Mid-Atlantic ridge

timeline (million years ago)

Level 7

14 Sam has three metal bars. One is aluminium, one is iron and one is a magnet. Explain how Sam can work out which is which using another magnet.

15 Because he could not go into space, William Gilbert used a model of the Earth to find out if it had a magnetic field. For what other reasons might someone use a model to test something?

16 Suggest what the effect will be if you pass the current along an electromagnet in the opposite direction.

17 What evidence have you found that the poles are due to flip again?

The Grand Canyon in Arizona, USA, is 446 km long, up to 29 km wide and 1.6 km deep. It was created by the Colorado River carving its way through the desert landscape.

Geologists are scientists who study rocks and the Earth, and they have spent a lot of time studying the Grand Canyon. The Grand Canyon is important because it has lots of different kinds of fossils, a variety of rock types and different geological features. Scientists can also see clearly the different layers of rock that have been created at different times in the Earth's history. These rocks and the fossils they contain provide geologists with evidence of how life on Earth evolved.

In recent years, advances in technology have made it possible for geologists to work out the age of rocks. This also helps them to predict volcanic eruptions and earthquakes. These developments are important as many millions of people live near volcanoes and in earthquake zones.

Now try these

- Make a list of the different types of rocks you know.

- Write down as many uses of rocks as you can think of.

- Suggest why a gravestone from 1810 is much more difficult to read than a gravestone from 1950.

Coming up in this Chapter ...

...un, wind and rain has weathered ...e sphinx for 4000 years

Rivers around the world carry huge amounts of sediment

Lava is molten rock that is normally over 1000 °C

Fossils are plants or animals that have been preserved in rock

▲ The face of the Sphinx in Egypt has been worn away over the past 4000 years

Learn about:

- how water, temperature and wind affect rocks
- how rocks can be broken up by living things
- how data from monitoring stations can be used to preserve monuments

In 1990 scientists built the Campbell Scientific Weather Station at the back of the Sphinx. The weather station monitors air temperature, rainfall and the direction and speed of the wind. This information is important because it helps scientists to understand how the rocks that the Sphinx is made of are being damaged and what they can do to preserve such an important monument.

All rocks exposed on the Earth's surface can be broken down into smaller pieces by the weather, plants and animals. Scientists call this **weathering**. The Sphinx is being damaged by the weathering of the rock it is made from.

A Explain what is meant by the term weathering. (Level 4)

▲ You can see bits of rock at the bottom of the mountain. They have been broken off as a result of weathering

Peeling like an onion

Rocks can be weathered by water, the wind and changes in temperature. These are physical changes because the rocks have only been broken down and not changed into new substances. Scientists call this **physical weathering**.

In the desert, temperatures can be very hot during the day and very cold at night. During the day heat makes the rocks expand, while at night low temperatures make the rocks contract. The surfaces of the rocks expand and contract every day and every night with the changing temperatures.

Eventually the outer layer of the rock peels away like the layers of an onion. This type of weathering is called **exfoliation**.

Interesting fact

The highest mountain in Britain is Ben Nevis in Scotland. It stands 1343 m high and once used to be as high as Mount Everest in the Himalayas, which is over 8000 m. The rocks on Ben Nevis have been weathered and eroded over the past 400 million years.

B Explain why the weathering of rocks by changes in temperature is similar to peeling the outer layers of an onion. (Level 5)

Ice wedges

Jasmine goes to collect the milk from the front doorstep. It's freezing cold outside. The milk in the bottle has frozen and cracked the bottle. She asks her science teacher why.

'Milk is mostly made of water,' says Miss Jacobs. 'When water freezes, it expands by almost 10%. When the milk froze in the bottle it expanded so much the bottle burst apart.'

When water freezes in cracks or joints in rocks, it expands the crack like a wedge. Eventually this breaks the rock apart. This is called **freeze–thaw weathering**. Potholes in the road are formed by freeze–thaw weathering.

▲ Rocks like these will be worn down to grains of sand

C Look at the photos of the mountain on the previous page and the glass bottle. Explain how the pile of rocks at the base of the mountain was formed. (Level 6)

Wind power

Rocks can also be worn away by the wind, which can blow tiny grains of sand against the rock. Some people use this process to clean buildings. It is called **sand blasting** and uses pipes to force sand at high speeds against the walls. Over the past 4000 years the Sphinx has been weathered by a similar process. The prevailing winds are from the north west, so this side of the monument has suffered the greatest weathering.

▲ What made this bottle crack?

The power of roots

Birds and animals drop seeds into cracks in rocks. These cracks provide shelter and moisture that allow the plant to grow. As roots develop, the strength of the roots forces the rock apart. This is called **biological weathering**.

Trees often push up paving stones on city streets with their roots. Animals, such as molluscs, boring into rocks at the seashore can also cause rocks to break up.

◀ The roots of trees are extremely powerful and can push up paving stones and walls

D Explain why more biological weathering takes place where there are no extremes of temperature. (Level 7)

Keywords
biological weathering, exfoliation, freeze–thaw weathering, physical weathering, sand blasting, weathering

8.3 Dissolving rocks

Learn about:

- how acid rain forms
- how acid rain affects rocks
- how scientists are collaborating to tackle acid rain

▲ Limestone (left) and granite (right) gravestones

> Look at the differences between these two gravestones. One is more worn away than the other, but they are both the same age.

Class 8c are doing a project on family histories. Becca and Sam have gone to the graveyard of the local church to look at gravestones.

> Perhaps they are made of different types of rock.

There are lots of different types of rocks, and they are made up of different minerals that come together like the ingredients in a cake. Gravestones are often made from **granite** or **limestone**. Granite is made up of three different coloured minerals that give it a speckled appearance, while limestone is made up of a single mineral called calcite (the mineral name for calcium carbonate).

Acid in the rain

Rain is a weak acid. When it passes through polluted air it becomes more acidic and it turns into **acid rain**. Calcite reacts with acid. When acid rain falls on limestone, it starts to dissolve and a new substance is made which is soluble in water. This is a chemical reaction – chemical changes take place in the rocks. Scientists call this type of weathering **chemical weathering**.

Limestone reacts easily with acid rain so you can see the effects of acid rain on statues, gravestones and buildings made from limestone. Some of the minerals in granite react slowly or not at all with acid rain, so granite is chemically weathered much more slowly than limestone.

You can see chemical weathering in the lab by comparing what happens when you drop dilute hydrochloric acid onto limestone and granite using a pipette.

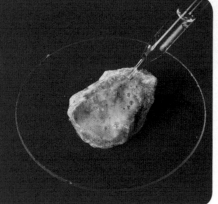

▲ Testing what happens when you drop hydrochloric acid onto limestone

▲ This statue has been chemically weathered by acid rain

A Explain why some rocks are more suitable than others to use for gravestones and statues. (Level 4)

B Explain why limestone is so easily affected by acid rain. (Level 5)

Controlling effects of acid rain

Pollution in the atmosphere comes from the burning of **fossil fuels** such as coal and oil. Pollution is greatest in cities but it can be carried great distances by the wind. Sometimes pollution is carried across to neighbouring countries which are not causing the pollution.

So what can scientists do about acid rain? Geologists and **environmentalists** monitor the effects of acid rain. The Department for Environment, Food and Rural Affairs (Defra) has set up stations on buildings and at the side of roads to monitor pollution. Chemists explain the causes of acid rain and recommend ways of reducing pollution.

These scientists work together and inform governments on the state of the atmosphere. Governments can then impose limits to control pollution.

C Explain why it is important that the government monitors pollution levels. (Level 6)

Reducing pollution

There are lots of ways that we can reduce pollution. Governments and industries often collaborate on ways to reduce pollution through improved technology.

- We can use cars less often, or we can use electric cars, or cars that are more fuel-efficient.
- We can improve public transport and use cleaner fuels (biofuels) for buses and trains, e.g. hydrogen-fuelled buses.
- We can put filters that remove pollution into vehicle exhausts and factory chimneys.
- We can use biofuels or renewable sources of energy to make electricity.

All of these technological improvements result in a decrease in the use of coal and oil, which produce polluting gases, and use alternative sources of energy that are cleaner and non-polluting.

D Using your knowledge of what is produced when calcium carbonate reacts with acid, explain why chemical weathering itself adds to pollution. (Level 7)

▲ Pollution-monitoring stations can be found on many busy UK roads. They measure the levels of pollution from vehicles

Interesting fact

Grotte Bournillon in France has the largest cave entrance in Europe. It is 80 m high. The cave has been made by acidic rainwater dissolving limestone under the ground.

Keywords
acid rain, chemical weathering, environmentalist, fossil fuel, granite, limestone, pollution

8.4 Rocks on the move

Learn about:
- what causes landslides
- how weathered fragments of rock are transported
- how engineers can reduce the effects of landslides

Landslide kills forty

In February 2007, heavy rain caused tonnes of mud and rocks to slide down a hillside on Flores Island in Indonesia. This is called a landslide. Lots of houses were washed away and 40 people were killed.

After rocks have been weathered, fragments of rock fall to the ground. Then they are usually moved somewhere else. The word that scientists use to describe rocks being moved is **transport**. Rocks can be transported in lots of different ways.

Scientists call the combination of the processes of weathering and transporting rocks at the Earth's surface **erosion**.

Gravity and rocks

The **landslide** on Flores Island was caused by gravity making part of the hillside move suddenly downhill. The very wet weather had loosened the soil and rocks.

Engineers can reduce or prevent the effects of landslides by:
- improving drainage so that water doesn't loosen the soil
- making slopes more stable
- building walls to protect houses
- diverting the paths of landslides.

▲ Gabions are piles of rock held together by wire mesh. They hold soil back, but let water pass through and so reduce the risk of a landslide

A Explain what caused the landslide on Flores Island. (Level 4)

Wind and water

The wind can't carry large, heavy fragments of rock, but it can carry small, light grains of sand. Strong winds can carry larger grains of sand.

A lot of weathered rock is transported away from hills and mountains by rivers. Near the source, which is where the river starts, the gradient is steep and large boulders are easily transported along the river bed. Closer to the mouth, or end of the river, the gradient is less and only finer sediment such as sand and mud is being transported.

B Which is likely to be carried furthest by a river – a large fragment of rock or a grain of sand? Explain your answer. (Level 5)

Ice

A **glacier** is a river of ice that moves very, very slowly. As a glacier moves, fragments of rock are broken off from the valley floor and sides and carried along. Glaciers can transport large boulders as well as fragments of rock and sand.

Wearing away

When rock fragments are transported by water and wind, they usually knock against each other. This means that their sharp edges and corners are worn away so that they become smaller and rounder. Rock fragments carried by glaciers keep their sharp edges. This is because they don't bump against each other while they are carried by the ice.

Rock fragments are eventually broken down into small pebbles, sand and soil. These are called **sediments**.

◀ A glacier is made of compacted snow. It forms high in the mountains and moves slowly down the valley by gravity

 C Explain what happens to a fragment of rock the longer it is transported. (Level 5)

Dumped!

When a river slows down, the transported material sinks to the bottom of the river because the river can't carry it along any more. This is known as **deposition**. This often happens at the mouth of a river where it meets the sea because there is less energy in the sea to transport the sediment away than there was in the river. The sediment can build up to form a flat, marshy area called a **delta** where it meets the sea.

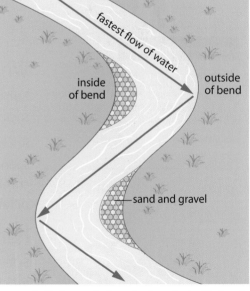

▲ Sediment is deposited on the inside bend of the river where there is less current

 D Explain why there is a lot of sediment at the mouth of a river but much less near its source. (Level 6)

E Look at the diagram showing sediment being deposited on a bend in a river. What does this tell you about the speed of the water around the bend? (Level 7)

Keywords
delta, deposition, erosion, glacier, landslide, sediment, transport

8.5 Let's rock

Learn about:

- what rocks are made of and their properties
- how scientists' decisions affect the environment

▲ Understanding the properties of different rocks is essential if you are building a reservoir

Interesting fact

Building the Three Gorges Dam in China involved moving over 1.5 million people to clear space for the rising water. It will generate 22 500 Megawatts of power, enough to run 11 million homes.

Before building dams and reservoirs, engineers must study the local rocks. Dams and reservoirs should only be constructed where suitable rocks exist. A dam is the wall that holds back a lake of water, which is called the reservoir. Rocks around dams should be strong to carry the pressure of large volumes of water. The rocks should not contain any lines of weakness, called faults. The rocks along a fault can move with increasing pressure.

A Why should the rocks below a reservoir not contain any faults? (Level 4)

Hardness of minerals	
Mineral	**Mohs' hardness scale**
quartz	7
olivine	6.5
feldspar	6
calcite	3
black mica	2

What are rocks?

Rocks are essential to everyday life. We use rocks or the materials found in rocks to build aircraft and watches, cars, roads and bridges.

Rock is a solid, non-living material that occurs naturally. You have already seen that rocks are made up of lots of different minerals. Different combinations of minerals make different rocks and different rocks have different strengths.

Hardness

Scientists look at the **hardness** of different rocks. The hardness of a particular rock depends on what minerals are in the rock. Scientists all over the world measure the hardness of minerals against **Mohs' scale**. This is a scale ranging from 1 to 10, where diamond, the hardest known mineral, has a hardness of 10 and talc, which is a very soft mineral, has a hardness of 1. The table on the left shows the hardness of some minerals.

B Look at the data in the table. Which mineral is softer than calcite? (Level 5)

Rock texture

Some rocks are made of **grains** and some are made of **crystals**. The texture of a rock depends on how the grains or crystals are arranged inside it.

Density

Density is a measure of how heavy rocks are. Density is measured by weighing a rock and then working out its volume. The weight is then divided by the volume to give density. Rocks that have tightly packed **interlocking** crystals will have a higher density than rocks with loosely packed grains.

▼ Granite

grains of sand

pore space

interlocking of crystals

▶ Sandstone

C Explain why granite would provide a better site than sandstone for the construction of a reservoir. (Level 5)

Spongy rocks

Rocks which have a **non-interlocking texture** can absorb water or let water drain through them. Scientists call them **porous** or **permeable** rocks. Porous rocks can also hold air or oil. Rocks with an interlocking texture don't hold water or let water drain through them and scientists call them **non-porous** or **impermeable** rocks.

Amber and Sam weigh three different types of rocks and then put them into water. In their next lesson, they take the rocks out of the water and weigh them again. The table shows their results.

D Look at the data in the table. Which rock is a porous rock? Explain your answer. (Level 6)

How can we find out whether a rock is porous or impermeable?

Why don't we put different samples of rock into water? If a rock is porous, it will absorb water.

Rocks and water

Type of rock	Mass before soaking in water (g)	Mass after soaking in water (g)
granite	25.8	25.8
sandstone	22.6	25.1
marble	23.2	23.2

E Some rocks are more porous than others. If you had to compare the porosity of two rocks, one porous and one impermeable, explain how you could use the water experiment to do this. (Level 7)

When it rains, porous rocks can absorb water. This stops water collecting on the surface of the ground and causing floods. Oil wells are drilled into porous rocks that have trapped the oil in the tiny spaces between their grains.

By combining all the information on rocks in an area, geologists can decide whether dams can be built.

Keywords
crystal, grain, hardness, impermeable, interlocking, Mohs' scale, non-interlocking, non-porous, permeable, porous, texture

8.6 Hot rocks

Learn about:

- what igneous rocks are and how they are formed
- that evidence from the appearance of rocks can be used to predict how they were formed

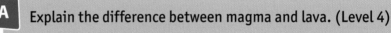

▲ Fast-flowing lava and clouds of hot ash are a major threat to people living on the slopes of an active volcano

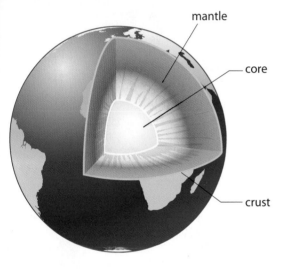

mantle

core

crust

▲ Inside the Earth

In January 2008, thousands of people were evacuated from villages near the Tungurahua **volcano** in Ecuador as it began to **erupt**, sending ash and **lava** into the air. Because of the devastation they cause, scientists need to understand how volcanoes form and how to predict when they might next erupt.

Igneous rock

Scientists have found enough evidence to be sure that the Earth is made up of different layers. The thin, outer layer is solid and is called the **crust**. Underneath the crust is a thick, partly **molten** (liquid) layer called the **mantle**.

Magma is hot liquid rock beneath the Earth's surface. When it erupts through a volcano it is known as lava. **Igneous rocks** are made from magma or lava that has cooled down and turned into solid rock.

> **A** Explain the difference between magma and lava. (Level 4)

Inside igneous rocks

Igneous rocks are made of crystals of minerals. They are hard rocks. The crystals form when the hot liquid magma or lava cools down and crystallises to form a rock. Different kinds of igneous rocks have different sizes of crystals. Some rocks have crystals that are a few centimetres long while other rocks have crystals which are just a few hundredths of a millimetre.

The size of the crystals depends on how long the magma or lava takes to cool down. **Extrusive** igneous rocks such as lava usually cool quickly on the Earth's surface and form rocks with small crystals, e.g. **basalt**.

Sometimes magma doesn't reach the Earth's crust and cools slowly deep underground, forming **intrusive** rocks with large crystals, e.g. **granite**.

▲ Basalt has small crystals. It forms when lava cools quickly

B Some igneous rocks cool deep in the crust, and others cool at the surface. What differences would you recognise between these rocks? (Level 5)

C If scientists could predict the possible eruption of a volcano, what measures could be taken to reduce loss of life? (Level 6)

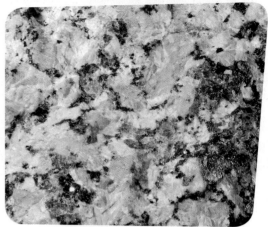

▲ Granite has large crystals. It forms when magma cools slowly

Different colours

Different kinds of igneous rock have a variety of colours because they are made up of different minerals. Light coloured igneous rocks contain a lot of silica and not very much iron. Dark coloured igneous rocks contain a lot of iron and less silica.

Volcanoes containing magma that is rich in silica produce thick lava that flows slowly. Volcanoes containing magma that is rich in iron produce thinner lava that flows quickly. They also erupt more frequently.

D Look at the photos of basalt and granite. Which rock is rich in silica? (Level 6)

Investigating crystals

You can model the effect that slow cooling or fast cooling has on crystal size in igneous rocks by melting a substance called salol in a test tube and then pouring a few drops onto a cold microscope slide and a few drops onto a warm microscope slide.

▲ Granite has an attractive 'spotty' appearance. It is often used for expensive designer kitchens

▼ Large crystals on warm slide

▲ Small crystals on cold slide

Interesting fact

Granite is an extremely hard rock which makes it very useful. The Ancient Egyptians used granite to make pyramids and tombs. Scientists don't know how they managed to cut it.

E Explain how the salol experiment above can be used to model cooling rates and the sizes of the crystals in igneous rocks. (Level 7)

Keywords
basalt, crust, erupt, extrusive, igneous rock, intrusive, lava, magma, mantle, molten, volcano

8.7 Layered rocks and fossils

Learn about:

- sedimentary layers
- what sedimentary rocks are and how they are formed
- how fossil evidence is used to date rocks

▲ The layers of sedimentary rock in this cliff are called strata and were formed as sediment was deposited

Fragments of rock are transported by water, wind and ice and deposited somewhere else as sediment. Over millions of years, this sediment builds up in layers in rivers, lakes, oceans and deserts. Scientists call these layers **sedimentary layers**.

When you look at sedimentary layers the oldest layers are at the bottom because they were deposited first. Different layers are made by different sediments.

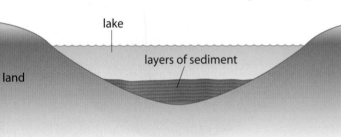

▲ How sedimentary layers form

Making rock

As the sedimentary layers become thicker, the grains of sediment at the bottom are squashed as a result of all the pressure of the sediment above. This is called **compaction**.

Compaction also squeezes air and water out of the sediment. There are often chemicals dissolved in this water. When the water is squeezed out, the dissolved chemicals that are carried in the water form crystals which are left behind. These crystals stick the grains of sediment together – this is called **cementation**.

The sediment grains continue to be squashed and stuck together until the spaces between the grains are filled and **sedimentary rock** is formed.

Interesting fact

Sedimentary rocks like limestone were used to make many of the well known buildings in cities like London and Paris.

 A Name four environments on the Earth's surface where sedimentary rocks form. (Level 4)

What are sedimentary rocks like?

There are lots of different sedimentary rocks and they are made from different minerals. But sedimentary rocks made from the eroded fragments of other rocks all have some things in common:

- they have grains which are held together by 'cement'
- some have air spaces between their grains so they are porous
- they build up in layers on the Earth's surface.

Clues in the rocks

Geologists study the rocks and structures of the Earth. The size of sediment grain in a sedimentary rock can tell a lot about what the environment was like when the sediment was being deposited.

If the grains in a sedimentary rock are mostly pebbles, then the pebbles were transported in fast-flowing water. If the grains are mostly sand-sized, then the environment might have been a beach or a desert. Very tiny grains usually mean that the sediment was deposited somewhere very calm, like a lake.

Some sedimentary rocks

Name	What it looks like	What it is made from
limestone		calcium carbonate grains – often from bits of shells
sandstone		quartz grains
chalk		very fine grains of calcium carbonate
shale		fine, compressed mud

B What similarities and differences can you see between limestone and chalk in the table on the right? (Level 5)

C Look at the data in the table. (i) Suggest what type of environment chalk was formed in. (ii) Do you think that chalk and limestone were formed in different environments? Explain your answer. (Level 6)

Dating rocks

An engineer called William Smith constructed a system of canals across Britain in the late 1700s. He had to study the rocks before digging the canals to make sure his routes were suitable. He began to collect **fossils** from the sedimentary rocks.

Smith noticed that the fossils in a section of sedimentary rock were always in the same order from the top to the bottom. He also discovered that certain fossils could be found in a particular rock type in many different parts of Britain.

He realised that fossils could be used to date sedimentary rocks across a wide area. He was the first person to use fossil evidence to draw maps showing where the older and younger rocks are.

▲ The different colours on William Smith's map show different kinds of rocks

D Ammonites are extinct marine organisms and their fossils can be found all over the world. How can these fossils be used to date rocks on different continents? (Level 7)

Keywords
cementation, compaction, fossil, sedimentary layer, sedimentary rock

139

8.8 Changing rocks

Learn about:

- how temperature and pressure can change one rock type into another

The Alps are mountains in central Europe

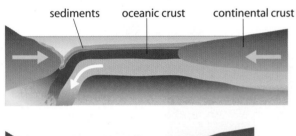

sediments   oceanic crust   continental crust

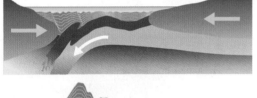

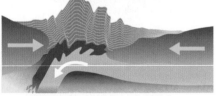

▲ Great pressures in the Earth's crust deform the rocks into a series of folds, making the rock layers look crumpled

Mountains like the Alps are forced up by great Earth movements over millions of years. The Alps are made of **metamorphic rocks** that began as sediments on the seabed.

'Metamorphosis' means changing from one form to another. Metamorphic rocks are formed when sedimentary rocks have been changed by heat or a combination of heat and pressure.

Hot, squashed rocks

Most metamorphic rocks form because of intense heat and pressure on sedimentary rocks. This happens deep beneath the Earth. Rocks are also subjected to high temperature and pressure at the edges of plates when they are pushed together. This results in a change in appearance of the rocks.

The rocks don't actually melt but the minerals in the rocks change chemically. The new minerals form as crystals, making metamorphic rocks. The pressure makes the crystals line up. This is why some metamorphic rocks often have layers or bands in them. Also, the crystals in metamorphic rocks are usually interlocking so they are not porous.

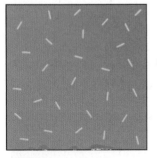

pressure   pressure

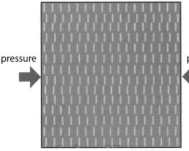

before pressure the minerals are random. Heat and/or pressure change the minerals into new ones

when pressure is applied to the rock the crystals line up in layers

A Explain how sedimentary rocks can be changed into metamorphic rocks. (Level 4)

B Explain why some metamorphic rocks have layers in them. (Level 5)

Baked rock

Metamorphic rocks can also be formed from rocks that are 'baked' when they are near heat. This can happen near a volcano where the hot magma heats the rocks nearby and changes them.

Sandstone is made up of grains of quartz which become interlocking crystals under lots of heat and pressure. This new rock is called quartzite, which is a very hard rock.

 C Explain why metamorphic rocks can be found close to volcanoes. (Level 6)

Different metamorphic rocks

There are lots of different metamorphic rocks. The type of metamorphic rock you find depends on which sedimentary rock it started out as. You have already seen that limestone changes into marble, while sandstone becomes quartzite.

The amount of heat and pressure also affects what kind of metamorphic rocks are produced. By looking at the photos, see what happens when sedimentary mudstone is subjected to different amounts of heat and pressure.

D Explain how the intensity of heat and pressure responsible for the formation of a metamorphic rock can be worked out by looking at the features of slate, schist and gneiss. (Level 6)

E Explain why the appearance and texture of a metamorphic rock give geologists clues about what happened to it. (Level 7)

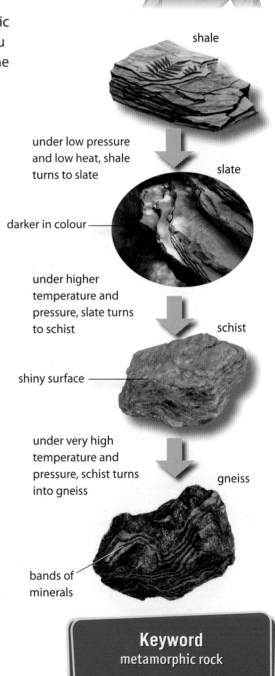

shale

under low pressure and low heat, shale turns to slate

slate

darker in colour

under higher temperature and pressure, slate turns to schist

schist

shiny surface

under very high temperature and pressure, schist turns into gneiss

gneiss

bands of minerals

Keyword
metamorphic rock

Summary of the three rock groups

Rock type	Texture	Formation	Uses
igneous rocks	interlocking crystals	cooling of molten magma	road stone and construction
sedimentary rocks	grains of sediment; some sedimentary rocks are porous, e.g. sandstone	weathered and eroded fragments of other rocks	statues and building stones
metamorphic rocks	interlocking crystals; some metamorphic rocks are banded	changed by heat and pressure	roofing industry and decorative products

8.9 Recycling rocks

Learn about:

- how the three rock types are linked
- how the rock cycle theory was accepted

▶ This landscape is the result of many different rock types

We now know a lot about how different rocks are formed. But how does it all fit together?

Igneous rocks are formed from rocks that have been melted, and sedimentary rocks are formed from the weathered remains of other rocks.

And metamorphic rocks are made from sedimentary rocks that have been heated, or heated and squashed.

All rocks on the Earth are recycled from other rocks. Rocks are continually and slowly changing from one type to another. This is known as the **rock cycle**. The processes in the rock cycle can take millions of years. We can see some of the surface processes in action, such as weathering or lava cooling to form igneous rock, but we can't see the processes operating deeper in the Earth's crust.

A Explain what is meant by the rock cycle. (Level 4)

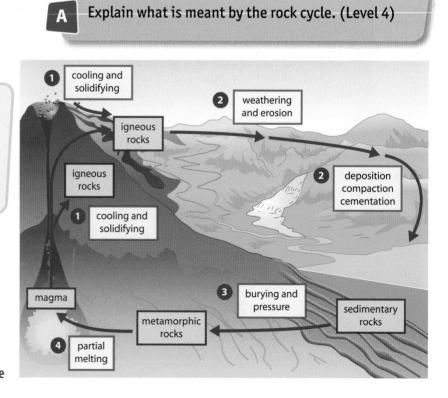

1 cooling and solidifying

2 weathering and erosion

igneous rocks

2 deposition compaction cementation

igneous rocks

1 cooling and solidifying

magma

3 burying and pressure

sedimentary rocks

metamorphic rocks

4 partial melting

▶ The rock cycle

The rock cycle on the previous page can be divided into four stages:

Stage 1: Igneous rocks are the first rocks formed in the rock cycle. They are formed from magma that cools inside the Earth's crust or lava that cools at the surface.

Stage 2: Once rocks are formed, they are weathered and eroded over millions of years. The sediment formed is transported, deposited and eventually becomes compacted and cemented to form sedimentary rocks.

Stage 3: Some sedimentary rocks are subjected to great pressure deep in the Earth and are changed into metamorphic rocks.

Stage 4: When these metamorphic rocks are pushed deeper into the Earth, temperatures and pressures are at their highest. The rocks melt, forming magma, and the cycle starts all over again.

B Using the rock cycle diagram, make a flowchart to explain how igneous rocks become metamorphic rocks. (Level 5)

C Some of the processes within the rock cycle occur on the surface and some below the surface. Separate these two groups of processes into a table. (Level 6)

D You could use layers of plasticine as a model for the formation of sedimentary rocks. (i) Is this a good model? Explain your answer. (ii) What could you do to the layers of plasticine to model the formation of metamorphic rocks? (Level 7)

Accepting a theory

James Hutton (1726–1797) was a Scottish scientist who studied rocks. Lots of people think that he was the father of modern geology. He studied rocks all over Scotland and came up with a theory that what happens to rock happens in cycles and that there are lots of cycles over millions of years.

His theory was not accepted for many years. A new theory explaining how parts of the crust move was developed by a scientist in the 1960s and 1970s. This provided some of the final evidence for Hutton's theories.

▲ James Hutton first came up with the idea of the rock cycle

Keyword
rock cycle

8.10 Studying volcanoes

Learn about:

- why scientists study volcanoes
- how scientists collect data from volcanoes
- the dangers of studying volcanoes

▲ Today Vesuvius is dormant, but it could become active at any time in the future

Lots of people today live on the slopes of active volcanoes. The soil near volcanoes is very fertile so many of these people are farmers. Large cities have also grown up near some of these volcanoes despite the threat of an eruption. The city of Naples is close to Vesuvius, and several cities in Japan lie in the shadow of Mount Fuji.

Eruption!

When a volcano erupts, large amounts of ash and gases such as sulfur dioxide can be produced. Hot lava can pour out, covering everything in its path.

The diagram shows a cross-section through a volcano. Sticky lava sometimes cools and forms a solid plug in the **vent** of the volcano which blocks it. This causes pressure to build and a new eruption will begin with a violent explosion, often with large volumes of ash and gases that travel at great speed and sometimes over long distances. This is very dangerous and is called a **pyroclastic flow**. The ash from pyroclastic flows can pollute water supplies, cause breathing problems in humans and animals and destroy crops and vegetation.

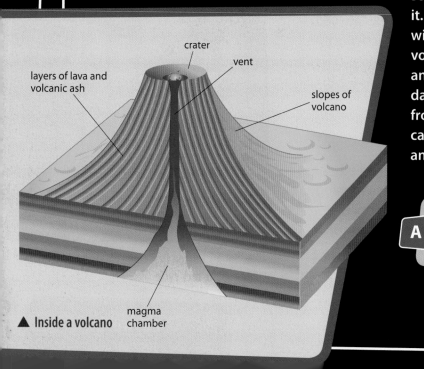

crater

vent

layers of lava and volcanic ash

slopes of volcano

magma chamber

▲ Inside a volcano

A Explain why people live near active volcanoes even though they are dangerous. (Level 4)

B Explain how pressure causes explosive eruptions. (Level 5)

Studying volcanoes

Scientists who study volcanoes are called **volcanologists**. They study volcanoes so they can understand more about how they work and what happens when volcanoes erupt. This knowledge is vital for predicting when a volcanic eruption might happen, so people living near the volcano can be warned and evacuated from the area.

Volcanologists collect lots of data from volcanoes that can be used to predict an eruption:

- They collect gases from vents or by flying an aircraft above the crater to monitor what kinds and amounts of gases are being produced by the volcano.
- They set up instruments called **seismometers** that record earthquakes resulting from rising magma in the vent.
- They measure the temperature changes of volcanic vents and use satellite thermal images to map the temperature in the crater.
- They collect data on the previous lava flows, ash fallout and blast damage.

Using aircraft and satellite images is safer than attempting to collect data at ground level. The data collected and records of previous eruptions are used by volcanologists to draw **hazard maps**. These maps predict the paths of possible lava flows.

Staying safe

Volcanologists spend many years studying different volcanoes. Many, like Maurice and Katia Kraft, have died during volcanic eruptions. Methods of volcanic prediction are improving with modern scientific techniques, but collection of data directly from craters will always be dangerous. Conditions within a volcano can change quickly and an eruption can occur without warning.

▲ Pyroclastic flows can travel at up to 150 mph

Scientists at work

The French volcanologists Maurice and Katia Kraft produced an information film about the dangers of living close to volcanoes. This has been used in lots of countries to make people aware of the dangers and how to react to them.

▲ Collecting data on a volcano can be very dangerous

C A volcano erupts and volcanologists draw a hazard map of the area likely to be affected by ash and lava flows.
(i) Explain how this hazard map can help them to predict what will happen the next time the volcano erupts.
(ii) Suggest what might happen to make their prediction wrong. (Level 6)

D Evaluate the levels of danger to volcanologists when collecting their data. (Level 7)

Keywords
hazard map, pyroclastic flow, seismometer, vent, volcanologist

8.11 MAROONED ON A ROCKY ISLAND

Learn about:

- how to use your knowledge about rocks to find water

Best Science Lesson Ever

Written by the National History Museum with the Earth Science Education Unit

NATURAL HISTORY MUSEUM

Ryan, Becca, Amber, Sam and Jasmine have been washed up on a rocky island in the middle of the Pacific Ocean. They know that help will be on its way but they have to survive on the island for several days until they are rescued.

Luckily they spot an old abandoned hut on the beach that must have been used by geologists who recently surveyed the island.

Inside the hut

When they explore the hut, they find a number of different things:

- a view of the island from the beach
- some field notes
- dehydrated meals

▲ **If you were stranded on an island, would you know where to find water?**

Don't drink the water from the rivers — it isn't clean and will cause sickness.

The only safe water is from the spring.

When it rains, water sinks into some of the rocks.

Water leaks out in a spring where permeable rock meets impermeable rock.

A   Explain why water soaks into some rock and not others. (Level 4)

Finding water

You can see from the field notes that the water from the rivers isn't safe to drink, and they can't drink seawater, so you need to help Ryan and his friends find a source of pure fresh water from a spring. Then they will be able to drink the water and rehydrate the meals in order to survive. The drawing on page 147 shows the view of the island from the beach.

Testing the rocks

Divide yourselves into small groups. Each group will need:

- different samples of sedimentary, metamorphic and igneous rocks
- beakers
- top pan balance
- paper towels
- stop watch

You are going to test a sample of each type of rock (sedimentary, igneous and metamorphic) to find out which one(s) soak up water (permeable) and which one(s) do not (impermeable).

Hazard Point | Sand View | Barren Top | Mighty Ramp | Crows Cliff

Igneous rock | Sedimentary rock | Metamorphic rock

What to do

1. Choose a type of rock to test.
2. Record the mass of the dry rock.
3. Predict what will happen to the mass of the rock once it has been placed in water.
4. Submerge the rock in water for 3 minutes, observe and record what happens.
5. Remove the rock from the water.
6. Dry the surface with a paper towel.
7. Find out the new mass.
8. Record your results in a table like the one here.
9. Repeat with the other types of rock.

Water test results

Type of rock	Mass of dry rock	What happens when rock is submerged in water	Mass of wet rock

B (i) Use your results to work out which types of rocks are permeable and which are impermeable. (ii) Look at the view of the island and work out where the spring is most likely to be found. Explain why. Do you think it will be at Hazard Point, Sand View, Mighty Ramp, Barren Top or Crows Cliff? (Level 5)

C Use drawings to show how rainwater can or cannot flow through each type of rock and explain why. (Level 6)

D As water enters the rock, what leaves the rock? How do your observations prove this? (Level 7)

Scientists at work

Mineralogists at the Natural History Museum study aspects of rocks, gems and minerals. Geologists study the origin, history and structure of the Earth.

Assess your progress

Level 4

1. Explain why limestone weathers more quickly than granite.
2. Name three ways that rocks can be weathered.
3. Explain the difference between weathering and erosion.
4. Explain why porous rocks are not suitable for reservoir construction.
5. Name four sedimentary rocks.
6. Explain the processes that change an igneous rock into a sedimentary rock.
7. Why is the work of a volcanologist dangerous?

Level 5

8. Explain why pot-holes in roads usually get bigger in winter.
9. Chemical weathering needs warm, damp conditions. Suggest two types of environment where chemical weathering would not happen very much.
10. Explain why most sediment is deposited at the mouth of a river.
11. Give two properties of granite and basalt that are similar and two that are different.
12. Oil is usually found in sedimentary rocks. Can you suggest why?
13. Put this list of rock types in order from the least to the most metamorphosed:

    gneiss   mudstone   slate

14. Write these stages in the rock cycle in the correct order, starting with volcanic eruption:

    weathering and erosion   deposition   rock melts
    sedimentary rocks form   burying and squeezing   volcanic eruption
    metamorphic rocks form   transportation
    igneous rock form   intense heat and pressure
    the whole cycle starts again

15. Some volcanoes erupt more explosively than others. Explain why.

Level 6

16 This strangely shaped rock is called a hoodoo.
The rock has been worn away by the wind. Suggest which part of the hoodoo
is made of hard rock and which part is made of soft rock.

17 Suggest reasons why sandstone increases in density after being soaked in
water.

18 Look at the diagram of igneous rocks A and B.

Which of the rocks was formed by molten
rock cooling slowly and which by molten rock
cooling quickly? Explain your answer.

19 What evidence did William Smith use to base
his geological maps on?

20 What changes take place when a sedimentary rock becomes a metamorphic rock?

21 Imagine you are a mineral just starting to form as you rise up out of a volcano and crystallise. Write
a report on your journey, explaining what happens to you as you move around all the stages of the
rock cycle.

22 Suggest measures that emergency services could use in the event of a volcanic eruption.

Level 7

23 Explain how pebbles of granite can be found in the sediment at the mouth of a river
even though there are no granite rocks nearby.

24 Explain why sandstone is more easily weathered than granite.

25 Imagine that you and your friends are particles in molten rock. When the teacher
shouts 'start cooling' you join hands with the person nearest to you, and in turn
each of you joins hands with the next nearest pupil. When the teacher says 'stop
cooling' you and your friends stay in the group that are holding hands and note the
size of the group. The experiment is repeated with less time between the teacher
shouting 'start' and 'stop'.

a How does this model show that slow cooling gives larger crystals?

b Suggest an improvement to the model.

26 A metamorphic rock made from a sedimentary rock doesn't have any fossils in it,
although the original sedimentary rock did have fossils. Explain why.

Science in the media

Learn about:

- how science is reported in the media
- how to evaluate the science being reported

LIFE IS SWEET

Scientists are now saying that eating lots of sweets is actually good for you. 'We have carried out a study which shows conclusively that eating sweets is good for your health.' says Dr Brian Sweetie of the Sweets Research Institute. 'We have evidence to prove that eating lots of sweets can help you concentrate and make your bones stronger.'

Samuel Fintry, the Managing Director of Goodsweets Manufacturing Ltd who sponsored the study, welcomed the news. 'We have said all along that sweets are good for you. Now we have proof.'

> Every day scientists are claiming to have proved or discovered something amazing.

> But can you believe everything that you read or see on the TV?

Where the information has come from

This report about sweets being good for you is imaginary. But every day we hear about real science on the news, read about it in newspapers or magazines, or view it on the Internet. Some sources of information are more reliable than others.

If the science is being reported on a national news programme or in a major newspaper, then the reporters will probably have checked the information to make sure it is correct. Information on the Internet isn't always checked. People often put information that is wrong or silly on their web pages. If you come across websites with the words 'alternative', 'alt' or 'unofficial' in their addresses then the information may not be correct.

▲ Official NASA website

▲ Joe Blogg's website Starzrcool

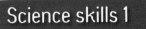

A Explain why the Internet isn't always a reliable source of information. (Level 4)

B Take a look at the NASA website and the Starzrcool website. Which one do you think is the more reliable source? Explain your answer. (Level 5)

Who has done the science?

You should consider whether a well respected scientist has carried out the research or investigation. You shouldn't accept everything that is written by someone who sounds like a scientist as being true. Most real science is carried out by teams of scientists and their findings are checked by other scientists before they are reported. This is called **peer review**.

C Sometimes scientific research is sponsored by companies that are trying to sell their products to the public. In the article on the previous page, Goodsweets Manufacturing Ltd sponsored the research into sweets. Is this likely to make the information in the article more or less reliable? Explain your answer. (Level 6)

▲ Scientists usually carry out research in teams and check each other's work

Is it good science?

When scientists carry out investigations, they are careful to follow **standard experimental procedures**. A standard procedure ensures that all scientists carry out the investigation in the same way. The results from their experiments are reliable and valid and the scientists make conclusions based on the evidence.

If an article or report does not tell you how an experiment or investigation was carried out, you should ask whether its conclusions are based on good scientific practice. Sometimes, articles on science are biased and only report the positive things about a discovery and not the negative things.

D A cosmetics company claims that its new brand of moisturiser will reduce wrinkles by 50%. This claim is based on 20 women testing the moisturiser for two weeks and reporting how they feel the moisturiser scores on a scale of 1 to 10. Is this is a valid scientific claim? Explain why or why not. (Level 7)

Keywords
peer review, standard experimental procedure

Writing about science

Learn about:

- researching information
- how to plan and write a report

▲ Being able to write a report is a useful skill in science

Look at the task

↓

What am I being asked to do?

↓

Who is the target audience?

↓

Plan report

▲ The process of creating a report

Scientists often write reports when they want to tell the world, and other scientists, about their discoveries.

You might be asked to write a report on an experiment or investigation that you have carried out, or you might be asked to research something and present an argument.

Class 8b have been asked to find out about nuclear power and write a report arguing whether it is a good thing or a bad thing. 'I'm going to the library to check out the books and magazines,' says Ryan. 'I'm going to look on the Internet,' says Sam. 'I bet there are lots of websites about nuclear power.'

When you do research you should keep a record of where your information comes from. You could use a table like this.

Recording your sources		
Question to be answered	Answer	Source – where the information came from

When you find information in books, magazines or on the Internet you should always ask yourself whether the information is relevant to the original question. Otherwise your report will be full of waffle. People often put incorrect information on websites so you need to think about whether the information you have found is accurate.

A Sam is going to research nuclear power on the Internet. What problems will Sam have in deciding which information to use? (Level 4)

Planning your report

Once you have done your research, you need to decide what you want to say in your report and the best way to say it.

When you are doing any kind of writing, you need to think about the people who are going to be reading it. They are called the **target audience** and they will affect the kind of language that you use. If you were a scientist writing for an academic journal you would use much more complex language than if you were writing for a children's science magazine. But whatever level of language you use, you need to be able to use scientific terms correctly in a science report.

> **B** Take a look at the two books. Who do you think their target audiences are? Explain your answer. (Level 5)

Writing your report

When you plan your report you need to decide how to order your ideas. Then you should organise them in a sequence of paragraphs that show your argument clearly. To help you do this, you need:

- an introduction to explain what the report is about
- the main part of the report with your ideas organised into paragraphs
- a conclusion to summarise your ideas.

It is a good idea to use a new paragraph for each new point that you make. For each paragraph:

- say what point you are making
- give the evidence that supports that point
- explain how the point and the evidence support your argument.

A good technique if you are arguing for or against something is to think of what your opponent might say. You can then point out why their argument is wrong. This is called a **counter-argument**.

Remember that you can use bullet points, diagrams, or charts and graphs in your report. Some things can be shown much more easily in a diagram than in words.

When you have finished writing your report, read it through and ask yourself:

- Have I done what was asked of me?
- Is everything relevant?

> **D** Sam wants to argue that nuclear power is a bad thing. (i) Suggest some points that he could use in his argument. (ii) He is going to include in his report Ryan's point that nuclear power doesn't add to air pollution. What counter-argument could he use against this? (Level 7)

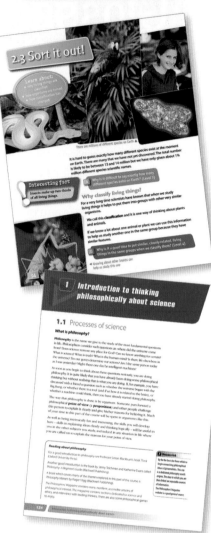

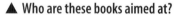
▲ Who are these books aimed at?

> **C** Ryan wants to argue that nuclear power is good because it doesn't add to air pollution. Would he be better to explain this in words or in a diagram? Explain your answer. (Level 6)

Keywords
counter-argument, target audience

Glossary

°C The unit of measurement of temperature.

absorption When light falls on an object and the energy goes into the object's surface so that none is reflected.

acid rain This is formed when rain passes through polluted air. The rain turns mildly acidic because of the pollution.

active immunity Immunity that develops when a person is exposed to a disease and produces their own antibodies to it.

aerobic respiration A form of respiration that requires oxygen to release the chemical energy in glucose for use by the cell.

agar plate A plate containing agar jelly used by scientists to grow bacteria.

AIDS A disease caused by the HIV virus which leads to weakening of the immune system. Short for **a**cquired **i**mmuno **d**eficiency **s**yndrome.

alveoli Tiny thin-walled air sacs in the lungs.

amplify To make a sound louder.

amplitude The amplitude of a sound refers to the size of the vibrations. A loud sound is produced by large vibrations, or in other words by a large amplitude.

amylase An enzyme that breaks down carbohydrates into smaller molecules.

anaerobic respiration A form of respiration that does not require oxygen to release the chemical energy in glucose for use by the cell.

anechoic chamber A chamber with soft padded walls that is designed not to produce echoes.

angle of incidence The angle at which a light ray arrives at a mirror, measured to the normal.

angle of reflection The angle at which a reflected ray leaves a mirror, measured to the normal.

angle of refraction The angle at which a ray travels after it has passed into a new material, measured to the normal.

anorexia An eating disorder that causes a person to eat too little.

antibiotic A drug that can kill bacteria but has no effect on viruses.

antibody A special chemical made by some white blood cells. Antibodies attach to microbes and help to destroy them.

antiseptic A weak disinfectant that is safe to use on human skin. Antiseptics kill microbes.

artery A blood vessel that takes blood away from the heart.

atom Small particle that makes up elements.

bacterium A type of microorganism, a single-celled organism much smaller than an animal cell and larger than a virus. Plural = bacteria.

balanced diet A diet that has the right amount of all the nutrients.

basalt Dark igneous rock, formed when magma cools quickly.

biological weathering The breakdown of rocks by plants and animals.

blood vessel Tubes in the body through which blood flows.

boiling point The temperature at which a liquid becomes a gas.

capillary Very small blood vessel linking arteries to veins.

carbohydrate Nutrient found in food such as bread that gives you energy.

carbolic acid The first disinfectant to be discovered.

cementation The process by which loose grains bond together – usually the cement is made from dissolved minerals carried in the water within the pore space of sedimentary rocks.

chemical property A characteristic of a chemical. The products of a reaction have different chemical properties from the reactants.

chemical weapon A chemical used in wartime to injure or kill people.

chemical weathering The breakdown of rocks by chemicals in the environment. The substances in the rocks are changed into new substances.

chlorophyll A green-coloured pigment that is found in leaves and is the chemical that enables photosynthesis to take place.

circulatory system An organ system that transports substances around the body.

cobalt A metal that can be magnetised.

cochlea Small snail-shaped container inside the ear that contains fluid and hair cells.

community A collection of plants and animals that share a habitat.

compaction The process by which grains within a sedimentary rock are pushed closer together because of the weight of the sediment above.

competition A situation where different organisms require the same resources.

compound A substance with more than one type of atom joined together.

conditioned stimulus A stimulus that is given alongside an unconditioned stimulus so that the two become linked or conditioned. It is 'learned'.

conditioning Training that links an automatic behaviour (reflex) to another behaviour which is not automatic.

conduction How energy is transferred through solids.

conductor (thermal) A material that lets heat pass through it quickly.

continuous variable A variable that can take any value along a scale, for example temperature.

convection How heat is transferred through liquids and gases.

convection current A circular movement of hot gases and fluids rising and cold gases and fluids falling.

counterargument An argument which explains why another argument is wrong.

coral reef A collection of small animals that form structures in the sea.

crust The solid outer layer of the Earth. The crust is the thinnest of the three layers.

crystal Regular shape formed by the arrangement of elements in a mineral.

cull To kill animals.

decibel The unit used to measure the loudness of a sound.

delta A flat area of land at the mouth of a river formed by deposition of sand and mud.

density How heavy an object is for its size.

dependent variable A variable that changes as a result of a change in an independent variable during an experiment or investigation.

deposition When a river dumps the material it is carrying, usually when the flow is slow.

diabetic A person who suffers from diabetes. Diabetics have a faulty pancreas that does not produce enough insulin.

diffuse Gas or liquid particles spreading out as their particles move and mix.

digestion The process by which food is broken down into smaller particles.

digestive juices Liquids in the digestive system that contain enzymes. These help to break down different nutrients.

digestive system The organ system that breaks down your food into smaller particles and then absorbs them.

disinfectant A strong chemical used to kill microbes.

dispersal When the colours of light separate to form a spectrum.

distillation A method used to separate mixtures of liquids with different boiling points.

E number Number code for a food additive that, following scientific tests, is currently thought to be safe. The E means 'edible'.

E. coli A type of bacterium.

ear canal Open tube leading from the centre of the ear flap to the eardrum.

eardrum A thin membrane stretched across the end of the ear canal that vibrates as sound waves enter the ear.

echoic chamber A chamber with hard, bare walls that is designed to produce a lot of echoes.

ecologist A scientist who studies the interaction between organisms and their environment.

ecosystem A complex community of plants and animals living in a specific part of the environment.

electromagnet A magnet that can be switched on and off using electricity.

element A substance that cannot be broken down into anything simpler.

environmentalist A person who cares for and studies the environment.

enzyme A substance that speeds up the breakdown of food in digestion.

erosion Loose pieces of rock are broken down while being transported.

erupt The process by which magma comes to the surface through a volcano.

evaporation Liquid turning into a gas by liquid particles absorbing energy.

exfoliation The breakdown of rocks by expansion and contraction as a result of daily temperature changes.

extrusive Igneous rock with small crystals, such as basalt; formed when lava cools quickly on the surface of the Earth.

fat Nutrient found in food, such as butter, that gives you energy and insulates your body.

fault A fracture in the Earth's crust along which two pieces of crust move.

fibre Bulky material found in cereals, fruits and vegetables that helps keep food moving through your gut.

food additive Any substance added to foods by food manufacturers. Different additives have different jobs – to colour, flavour or preserve the food.

fossil The remains of a once living organism or plant preserved within rock layers.

fossil fuel A material, made up of the remains of dead plants (coal) or animals (oil), which can be burnt to provide energy. Fossil fuels are non-renewable energy sources.

freeze–thaw weathering The breakdown of rocks by the continual freeze–thaw action of water and ice in cracks within rocks.

frequency The number of vibrations per second. The higher the frequency of a musical note, the higher the pitch.

fungus A type of organism that does not make its own food. It feeds on dead material. Some fungi are microorganisms.

gas A substance in which the particles are free to move.

gas exchange The movement of oxygen into the blood and carbon dioxide out of the blood. This takes place in the alveoli of the lungs.

gene A length of DNA that controls an inherited feature.

glacier A river of ice found in the valleys within high mountainous areas.

glucose A carbohydrate, which is also a sugar, that is used by the body to fuel respiration.

grain Eroded fragment of other rock that is found in sedimentary rocks.

granite Very hard igneous rock that forms when magma cools slowly. Often used as a building stone.

group One of the eight vertical columns in the Periodic Table.

gut The long tube in your body, between the mouth and the anus, down which food passes. This is where digestion and absorption take place.

habitat The place where an organism lives.

hardness The strength of a mineral based on Mohs' scale.

hazard map A map showing areas potentially affected by geological hazards, for instance areas destroyed if a volcano erupts lava or ash.

heart The muscular organ that pumps blood around the body.

heat A form of energy.

hertz (Hz) Unit of frequency used for measuring pitch.

HIV A virus which causes AIDS. Stands for **h**uman **i**mmunodeficiency **v**irus.

hypothesis A possible explanation for why something happens.

igneous rock A rock that has formed by the cooling of molten magma.

immune If you cannot get a disease you are said to be immune to it.

immune system The body's defences against disease.

impermeable A rock or material that will not allow liquids or gases to be held within it or to pass through.

infrared radiation Carries thermal energy from a hotter object to a cooler one.

insulator (thermal) A material that slows down the rate at which heat passes through it.

insulin A hormone produced by the pancreas that lowers the level of sugar (glucose) in the blood.

interdependent Different organisms in a population that rely on each other are said to be interdependent.

interlocking Crystals that have been fused together by heat, with no spaces between them.

intrusive Igneous rock with large crystals, such as granite; formed when magma cools slowly underground.

iron A metal that can be magnetised.

joule A unit of energy.

lactic acid The toxic product of anaerobic respiration.

landslide Rocks and mud slide down a slope under the effects of gravity, normally after a period of heavy rainfall or when the slope becomes unstable.

lava Molten rock from deep below the surface of the Earth that reaches the surface through cracks or volcanoes.

limestone Sedimentary rock made mainly of calcite.

line of best fit The line on a graph that shows the trend of the plotted data points. In science the line does not need to go through the data points.

lipase An enzyme that breaks down fats into smaller molecules.

liquid A substance in which the particles can slide over each other.

luminous Producing light.

lungs The pair of organs in the chest responsible for gas exchange.

magma Hot liquid rock beneath the surface of the Earth.

magnet A piece of magnetic material that can attract other magnetic materials.

magnetic field The space around a magnet where it attracts and repels.

magnetic field lines Lines that show the size, shape and strength of a magnetic field.

magnetism A non-contact force.

mantle The thickest layer of the Earth between the core and the crust.

melt Turn a solid into a liquid.

melting point The temperature at which a solid becomes a liquid.

metal A material that is usually solid and shiny when polished. A few are magnetic.

metallurgist A scientist who studies metals.

metallurgy The study of the physical and chemical properties of metals, and their uses.

metamorphic rock A rock formed when heat and pressure are applied to older sedimentary and igneous rocks, changing them into metamorphic rocks.

microbe Short for microorganism.

mineral (biology) Compound of calcium, iron or other elements that are needed in your diet in small amounts to keep you healthy.

mineral (geology) A naturally occurring substance. Rocks, such as limestone, are made up of minerals, e.g. calcite.

mixture A material that contains more than one substance.

MMR vaccine A vaccine that helps to protect children against getting **m**easles, **m**umps and **r**ubella.

Mohs' scale A scale used to determine the hardness of minerals.

molecule A group of atoms joined together.

molten Another word for liquid.

mould A type of fungus.

nickel A metal that can be magnetised.

non-interlocking Grains which are not in contact.

non-metal A material that is usually a solid or a gas. Non-metals have many different appearances.

non-porous A rock or material that does not hold liquids or gases.

normal An imaginary line that leaves the surface of a mirror at right angles. It is used as a reference line when describing rays coming to and from the mirror.

north pole A pole of a magnet that points towards the geographic North Pole of the Earth.

nuclear power The use of atomic energy to generate electricity.

nutrient Useful substance present in food.

nutritionist A scientist who studies nutrients in food.

obese People who are very overweight for their height.

observation Something which is noticed and recorded during an experiment or investigation.

opaque Made of a material that light cannot pass through.

oscilloscope An electrical device that represents a sound wave as a graph. Sounds can be detected using a microphone or generated by the machine.

pancreas An organ in the human body that produces digestive enzymes and hormones.

passive immunity Immunity which is given to a person through vaccination with ready-made antibodies.

pasteurise To treat with heat to destroy microbes, a process invented by the French scientist Louis Pasteur.

payback time The time it takes for the money saved by making an improvement to your home to cover the cost of making it.

peer review The process of scientists having their ideas or research evaluated by other scientists working in the same field.

penicillin An antibiotic drug found in a special mould.

period One of the seven horizontal rows in the Periodic Table.

Periodic Table A table containing all 113 elements, arranged by their properties in groups (columns) and periods (rows).

permeable A rock or material that allows the passage of liquids or gases.

photosynthesis The process by which plants produce glucose from carbon dioxide and water using the energy from sunlight.

physical weathering Breaking down rocks into small pieces without changing them into new substances. Physical weathering can be caused by water, wind and changes in temperature.

physiology The biological study of the function of living organisms.

pitch The pitch or frequency of a note depends on the number of vibrations per second. Higher pitched notes sound squeakier and correspond to more vibrations per second.

plasma A very hot electrically-charged gas.

pollution The contamination of the atmosphere, earth and water by human activities.

population The number of organisms of a certain species living in a habitat.

porous A rock or material that will hold liquids or gases.

product A new substance that is formed in a chemical reaction.

protease An enzyme that breaks down proteins into smaller molecules.

protein Nutrient found in food, such as fish and meat, that is used by your body for growth and repair.

psychologist A scientist who studies how people or animals behave.

pure A pure material contains only one substance.

pyramid of biomass A diagram showing the mass of each organism at each stage of a food chain.

pyramid of numbers A diagram showing the numbers of each organism at each stage of a food chain.

pyroclastic flow A cloud of hot ash, gas and rocks that travels down the side of a volcano at great speed.

radiation How energy travels without particles.

radiotherapy A process that uses high-energy radiation, e.g. X-rays, to kill cancer cells.

rainbow On a wet sunny day, we may see an arc of colour. It is an illusion, created by the refraction and reflection of sunlight in raindrops.

ray diagram A way to model how light behaves, using a diagram.

reactant A substance that takes part in a chemical reaction. It changes into the products.

reflect When light or sound or heat bounces off a surface, it is reflected.

relay A switch that uses an electromagnet.

resonance When an object picks up vibrations from something that is vibrating and starts to vibrate itself.

respiration The process by which all living things release the chemical energy in glucose in a controlled manner for cells to use.

respiratory system An organ system that takes oxygen into the body and gets rid of carbon dioxide from the body.

risk assessment A way of finding out how safe it is to do something, such as carrying out an experiment.

rock cycle The constant and never ending recycling of rocks by internal and surface processes.

sand blasting The effect on rocks of being hit by small particles of sand carried by the wind.

scurvy A disease caused by not eating enough vitamin C in the diet. The gums bleed and the skin does not heal.

sediment The material, such as sand and mud, that a river transports.

sedimentary layer A bed of sedimentary rock formed by deposition of sediment.

sedimentary rock A rock that forms in different environments on the surface of the Earth, usually from weathering and erosion of older rock.

seismometer The instrument used to detect and measure the strength of earthquakes.

small intestine The part of the gut where absorption of small food particles occurs. Most digestion occurs here.

solid A substance in which the particles are held together by forces.

south pole A pole of a magnet that points towards the geographic South Pole of the Earth.

standard experimental procedure An accepted and consistent way of carrying out an experimental procedure.

state of matter The three states of matter are solid, liquid and gas.

steel A metal alloy that can be magnetised.

stomach The part of the gut where food is churned up and mixed with some enzymes in acidic conditions.

symbol Sign representing an element, e.g. Fe is the symbol for iron.

target audience The people whom something such as a piece of writing is aimed at.

TB The abbreviation for the disease tuberculosis.

temperature The energy per particle.

texture The arrangement of grains or crystals in a rock.

theory A scientific explanation or model.

thermal energy The scientific term for heat.

translucent Made of material that lets light through but jumbles the light so that you can't make out objects on the other side.

transmission When light passes through an object.

transparent Made of material that allows light through it and through which you can see clearly.

transport The movement of sediment by water, wind, ice and gravity.

unconditioned stimulus A stimulus which provokes a reflex, e.g. a puff of air in the eye provokes blinking.

vaccinate To inject someone with dead or inactive microbes to make them immune to a disease before they catch it.

vaccine A mixture containing microbes that normally cause disease but which have been treated so that they are harmless. It is injected into people to make them immune to the disease.

vacuum A volume of space which contains nothing – not even air.

vein A blood vessel that takes blood back to the heart.

vent The cylindrical pipe in a volcano that connects the magma chamber and the crater.

virus The smallest type of microbe. Some scientists do not think that viruses are living because they do not carry out the processes of life for themselves and are not made of cells.

vitamin A substance that is needed in very small amounts to keep the body healthy. Vitamin C, which is found in fruit, is an example.

volcano A cone-shaped structure on the Earth's crust through which lava flows.

volcanologist A scientist who studies volcanoes.

weathering The breakdown of rocks by the weather, plants and animals.

white blood cell A blood cell that helps to fight microbes. It is a vital part of the immune system.

white light Light that contains all the colours of the rainbow.

word equation Shows what happens in a chemical reaction, using the names of the reactants and products.

yeast A type of fungus used in brewing and baking. It is a single-celled organism.

Index

Heinemann is an imprint of Pearson Education Limited, a company incorporated in England and Wales, having its registered office at Edinburgh Gate, Harlow, Essex, CM20 2JE. Registered company number: 872828

www.heinemann.co.uk

Heinemann is a registered trademark of Pearson Education Limited
Text © Pearson Education Limited 2008
First published 2008
Fourth impression 2009
12 11 10 09
10 9 8 7 6 5 4

British Library Cataloguing in Publication Data
A catalogue record for this book is available from the British Library.

ISBN 978 0 435503 71 0

Consulting editor: Carol Chapman, Head of Science, Selly Park Technology College for Girls

Produced by Wooden Ark

Original illustrations © Pearson Education Limited 2008

Illustrated by HL Studios and Dylan Gibson

Picture research by Beatrice Ray

Cover illustration by Skwak © Pearson Education Limited 2008

Printed in Italy by Printer Trento S.r.l

We endeavor to ensure that the paper and board used in our books has been made from pulp sourced from sustainable forests. We are also dedicated to working with printers who meet the highest environmental and employment standards.

Acknowledgements
We would like to thank the **Natural History Museum**, the **Earth Science Education Unit**, **Jonathan Hare, Helena Ward** and the **John Warner School, Hoddersdon** for their invaluable help in the development and trialling of this course.

The author and publisher would like to thank the following individuals and organisations for permission to reproduce photographs:

2 and 3, ©S.Carmona/CORBIS;3, **bottom, from L to R** ©A. Green/zefa/Corbis; ©Dick Makin/Alamy; ©Peter Evans; ©Bettmann/CORBIS; 4 , **T** ©ersoy emin/Alamy, **M** ©Photofusion Picture Library/Alamy, **B** ©St. Mary's Hospital Medical School/Science Photo Library; 5, ©iStockphoto/aristotoo; 6, **T** ©Alamy Images/Stock Image, **B** ©Colin Cuthbert/Science Photo Library; 7, ©ersoy emin/Alamy; 8, ©Bettmann/Corbis; 9, ©AJ Photo/HPR Bullion/Science Photo Library;10, ©Sally and Richard Greenhill/Alamy; 12, **T** ©Getty Images, **B** ©iStockphoto/Arne Trautmann; 14, ©Dominic Burke/Alamy; 15, ©Medical-on-Line/Alamy; 16, ©iStockphoto/Heike Loos, 18, ©geogphotos/Alamy; 22 and 23, ©CNRI/Science Photo Library;23, **bottom, from L to R** ©Garry Watson/Science Photo Library; ©Bettmann/Corbis; ©Jerome Delay/AP/PA Photos; ©Ashley Cooper/Corbis;24 , **T** ©James Cavallini/Science Photo Library, **M** ©David Scharf/ Science Photo Library, **B** ©Science Source/Science Photo Library;25 ,**TR** ©Jack Carey/Alamy, **Tab T** ©Dr Kari Lounatmaa/Science Photo Library, **Tab M** ©Scimat/Science Photo Library, **Tab B** ©Scott Camazine/CDC/Science Photo Library; 26, **T** ©iStockphoto/Mark Kostich, **B** ©Bettmann/Corbis; 27, **T** ©Bettmann/Corbis, **B** ©Pearson Education/Peter Morris; 28, **T** ©John Cole/Science Photo Library, **M** ©Science Photo Library; 29, ©Peter Gould; 30 , **T** ©Saturn Stills/Science Photo Library, **M** ©Eye Of Science/Science Photo Library; 31, ©Reuters/Corbis; 32, ©Frank Hormann/AP/PA Photos; 36 and 37, ©iStockphoto/Len Tillim; 37, **bottom, from L to R** ©Penny Tweedie/Alamy, ©iStockphoto/Edwin van Wier, ©blickwinkel/Alamy, ©iStockphoto/Roberta Casaliggi; 38, **TL** ©iStockphoto/Nikola Hrisnik, **TR** ©Garden World Images Ltd/Alamy; 39, **T** ©iStockphoto/David Lochhead, **B** ©iStockphoto/Andy Gehrig; 42 , **T** ©iStockphoto/Stefanie Timmermann , **M** ©blickwinkel/Alamy; 43, ©iStockphoto/Tammy Peluso; 44, **T** ©iStockphoto/iofoto, **M** ©iStockphoto/Joseph Manor, **B** ©Steve Bloom Images/Alamy; 45, **T** ©Bettmann/CORBIS, **B** ©PDSA/PA Archive/PA Photos; 46, ©Graham Uney/Alamy; 47, ©Andrew Linscott/Alamy; 50 and 51, ©NASA/Handout/CNP/Corbis; 51, **bottom, from L to R** ©Andrew Paterson/Alamy, ©Newmann/zefa/Corbis, ©National Archives and Records Administration, ©Chris Honeywell; 52, **T** ©Klaus Hackenberg/zefa/Corbis, **M** ©Martyn F. Chillmaid/Science Photo Library; 54, ©iStockphoto/David H. Lewis; 56, **TL** ©Bob Krist/CORBIS, **TR** ©iStockphoto/Steve Geer; 57, **L Tab T** ©Kaj R. Svensson/Science Photo Library, **L Tab TM** ©Klaus Guldbrandsen/Science Photo Library, **L Tab BM** ©Charles D. Winters/Science Photo Library, **L Tab B** ©Dirk Wiersma/Science Photo Library, **R Tab T** ©iStockphoto/Daniel Loiselle, **R Tab TM** ©iStockphoto/pxlar8, **R Tab M** ©Reed International Books Australia/Lindsay Edwards Photography, **R Tab BM** ©iStockphoto/Luis Albuquerque, **R Tab B** ©iStockphoto/Anthony Hall, **M** ©iStockphoto/Aliaksandr Niavolin; 58 ,**T** ©Francesco Ruggeri/Getty Images, **Tab T** ©Andrew Lambert Photography/Science Photo Library, **Tab TM** ©Andrew Lambert

Photography/Science Photo Library, **Tab BM** ©Charles D. Winters/Science Photo Library, **Tab B** ©Charles D. Winters/Science Photo Library; 59 , ©iStockphoto/Angus Forbes; 60, ©PhotoDisc/StockTrek; 61 ,**Tab L** ©Martyn F. Chillmaid/Science Photo Library, **Tab M** ©Andrew Lambert Photography/Science Photo Library, **Tab R** ©Maximilian Stock Ltd/Science Photo Library, **TR** ©Pearson Education/Trevor Clifford; 62, ©iStockphoto/Wolfgang Amri; 63, ©Andrew Lambert Photography/Science Photo Library; 64, ©Simon Fraser/Science Photo Library; 65 ©Getty Images; 66, **T** ©Carlos Cazalis/Corbis, **B** ©National Archives and Records Administration; 67, **T** ©Steve Starr/Corbis, **M** ©iStockphoto/Hans F. Meier, **B** ©Health Protection Agency/Science Photo Library; 70, ©Popperfoto/Getty Images; 71, ©James France; 71, **bottom, from L to R** iStockphoto/KateLeigh; ©Pearson Education/Rob Judges; ©PhotoDisc/StockTrek; ©NREL/US Department Of Energy/Science Photo Library; 72, ©PhotoDisc; 73 , **T** ©Digital Vision, **B** ©iStockphoto/Irochka Tischenko; 74, ©Science Photo Library; 75 , **T** ©James L. Amos, Peter Arnold Inc./Science Photo Library, **B** ©Nasa/Science Photo Library; 76, ©Bill Stormont/Corbis; 77, **T** ©iStockphoto/Elemental Imaging, **B** ©Andrew Lambert Photography/Science Photo Library; 78, ©iStockphoto/Alexandr Ozerov; 79, ©iStockphoto/Dmitry Kutlayev; 80, **T** ©Javier Barbancho/Reuters/Corbis, **B** ©Tony Mc connell/Science Photo Library; 81, **T** ©Andrew Holbrooke/Corbis, **B** ©iStockphoto/Joe Tamassy; 82, **T** ©NASA, **B** ©AFP/Getty Images; 83, ©NASA/JPL/Science Photo Library; 86 and 87, ©NASA; 87, **bottom, from L to R** ©iStockphoto/Nicola Stratford, iStockphoto/Joseph C. Justice Jr., ©Alex Bartel/Science Photo Library, ©Travelshots.com/Alamy; 88 , **T** ©Creatas, **B** ©Jerry Lodriguss/Science Photo Library; 89, **L** ©iStockphoto/Nicholas Belton, **R** ©Pearson Education/Jules Selmes; 90, ©AFP/Getty Images 91, ©Richard Smith; 92, ©iStockphoto/Jess Wiberg; 94, ©iStockphoto/Anton Gvozdikov; 95, ©iStockphoto/Michelle Malven; 96, **T** ©Photodisc, **B** ©Bettmann/Corbis; 97, **TL** ©Photodisc/Life File/Dave Thompson, **B** ©Science Museum/Science & Society; 99, ©Jonathan Hare; 100 and 101, ©iStockphoto/Stacey Griffin; 101, **bottom, from L to R** ©Paul Doyle/Alamy, ©Tim Cuff/Alamy, ©Rainer Holz/zefa/Corbis, ©iStockphoto/Lotfi Mattou; 102, **T** ©Hulton-Deutsch Collection/Corbis, **B** ©iStockphoto/iLexx; 103, ©iStockphoto/endrille/Andrey Armyagov;104 , ©Issei Kato/Reuters/Corbis; 105, ©Digital Stock; 106, ©Salford University; 108, ©James King-Holmes/Science Photo Library; 109, ©iStockphoto/James Steidl; 110, ©Photofusion Picture Library/Alamy; 111, ©Justin Kase zfivez/Alamy; 114 and 115, ©iStockphoto/Andrey Volodin; 115, **bottom, from L to R** ©iStockphoto/James Steidl, ©PhotoDisc, ©Simon Fraser/Science Photo Library, ©iStockphoto/Torsten Karock; 116, ©National Maritime Museum, London, UK/The Bridgeman Art Library; 117, ©iStockphoto/Andrew Howe; 118, iStockphoto/Constance Mcguire; 119, Photodisc/Stocktrek; 120, ©Corus Steel Packaging & Recycling; 121, ©John Mclean/Science Photo Library; 122, ©B. Murton/Southampton Oceanography Centre/Science Photo Library; 126 and 127, ©AFP/Getty Images; 127, **bottom, from L to R** iStockphoto/Franck Camhi, ©James Brunker/Alamy, ©iStockphoto/Julien Grondin, iStockphoto/asterix059;128, **T** ©iStockphoto/Spas Popov, **B** ©National Geophysical Data Center/John Lockridge;129,**T** ©Sinclair Stammers/Science Photo Library, **M** ©Martyn F. Chillmaid / Science Photo Library, **B** ©iStockphoto/dswebb; 130, **TL** ©Peter Jordan/Alamy, **TR** ©Stan Pritchard/Alamy, **B** ©Andrew Lambert Photography/Science Photo Library; 131, **T** ©Andrew Mcclenaghan / Science Photo Library; **B** ©Lourens Smak Alamy; 132, **T** ©AFP/Getty Images, **B** ©Gregory Dimijian/Science Photo Library; 133, ©iStockphoto/Debra McGuire; 134, ©Tina Manley/Industry/Alamy; 135, **TL** ©PhotoDisc, **TR** ©Joyce Photographics/Science Photo Library; 136, **T** ©National Geophysical Data Center/U.S. Geological Survey (R.E.Wilcox), **B** ©Mark A. Schneider/Science Photo Library; 137, **T** ©Jean-Claude Revy, Ism/Science Photo Library, **M** ©iStockphoto/Wayne Howard, **BL** ©Peter Gould, **BR** ©Peter Gould; 138, **T** ©PhotoDisc/Gary Irving; 139, **Tab T** ©Colin Keates/Dorling Kindersley, Courtesy of the Natural History Museum, London, **Tab TM** ©Joyce Photographics/Science Photo Library, **Tab BM** ©Mike Dunning/Dorling Kindersley, **Tab B** ©Harry Taylor/Dorling Kindersley, **B** ©British Geological Survey; 140, ©PhotoDisc/Martial Colomb; 141, **T** ©The Natural History Museum/Alamy, **TM** ©Brand X Pictures/Morey Milbradt, **BM** ©Doug Martin/Science Photo Library, **B** ©Andreas Einsiedel/Dorling Kindersley; 142, ©Brand X Pictures/Photo 24; 143, ©Science Photo Library;144, ©Cephas Picture Library Alamy;145, **T** ©Westend 61/Alamy, **B** ©Reuters/Corbis; 146, ©iStockphoto/Alberto Pomares; 150, ©Bubbles Photolibrary/Alamy; 151, ©Scott Bauer/Us Department Of Agriculture/Science Photo Library; 152, ©Andrew Fox/Alamy.

Every effort has been made to contact copyright holders of material reproduced in this book. Any omissions will be rectified in subsequent printings if notice is given to the publishers.